GGG O FLIP

GOD's
GREATEST
GIFT

OUR LORD

FELLOWSHIP WITH GOD
LORDS WORD
IRREVOCABLE IS GODS GIFT
PERSECUTED FOR OUR SALVATION

Tate Publishing & Enterprises

ACKNOWLEDGMENTS

I want to praise the Lord for giving me the insight and inspiration to write. My biggest supporters and fans, without question, are my soul mate and wife Deb and our children. Deb has shown me what true love is on this earth having the Lord as our guide. I want to thank all those who encouraged me to keep writing.

GGG O FLIP

TABLE OF CONTENTS

Help! I'm Stuck
How Dare You
How Do You Feel?
I Can Not Recall
I Can Not See It
I Didn't Know That
I Give Up
I Lost That Feeling
In Charge
It is all in the Timing
Judging
Just Passing Through
Justifying
Keep On Running
Life's Situations
Limits
Lonely
Look What I Found
Lord Please Help Me Too
Love You
Make it Quick
Masquerading
On the Run
One Trip Ship
Option Package
Over the Hill
Payday
Pieces of Stained Glass
Play on Words
Please Don't Give Up On Me
Please, Why?
Pleasing You

Pure Truth at This Location
Put Me In, I'm Ready
Quit Lying
Results
Self Service
Shining Through the Trees
Snake in the Hen House
Sponging
The 18-Inch Question
The Big Game
The Buffet
The Crossroads
The Doors
The Driver
The Fact of the Matter
The Getaway
The Pair Of…
The Path
The Pool
The Roof is Leaking
The Sky is Falling
The Slippery Step
The Stone or Rock
The Unknown Shopper
The Walking Billboard
This for That
This Side Up
Title
Tour Available Without Reservation
Toxic Mess
Visits

Wake Up Call
Walking on Water
Warning Whistle and Lights
Weeds on the Wire
Weekly Check Up
What does it feel Like?
What If?
What is the Awful Noise?
What Two Laws?
What's Your Problem?
Where Am I?
Where the Footsteps Go
Why do you not Answer Me?
Why do you Love Me?
Why Haven't You Learned?
Without Practice
Wouldn't That Be Great?

A Baby

We all start life as a baby. As a baby, we require nourishment in order to grow up to be strong and healthy. The time, love and patience given to us by our parents show us their unyielding love. When we are infants we cannot tell others what is wrong with us by words, therefore we communicate through our actions. The caring for us is a twenty-four hour a day, seven days a week responsibly until we can start to do things on our own. Our parents teach us right from wrong and influence us to seek the path of the Lord. When we reach the age of responsibility, we must choose our destiny. We are no longer infants and our choices are our own. When we accept Jesus Christ into our life, we become infants again. This time the Lord will show us the time, love and patience that were given to us by our parents. He will show us His unyielding love for us. He will forgive us for all our sins and show us the way to salvation and everlasting life. Our actions and thoughts will show the love we have for Him. May we show our babies the same love as the Lord shows us.

But I have stilled and quieted my soul; like a weaned child
with his mother, like a weaned child is my soul within me.
(Psalm 131:2) NIV

A Speck of Sand

Picture in your mind the most beautiful sunrise you have ever seen while you are sitting on a sandy beach. This is one of the thousands, if not more, of God's gifts to us. Viewing something this great is only the work of God; man or machine cannot recreate this. God's creation is not just by accident. Each piece of Gods' creation is for a reason. We may never know why but we do know there is a reason. Take a look at one speck of sand. We know that sand beaches are beautiful to look at or walk on. We know that people use sand to make glass and other products. However, what good is one speck of sand? Diseases! How can this be? Let's say you get one speck of sand in your eye, and you try to remove it but you can't. You go to the doctor for him to remove it. He notices that you may have glaucoma or cataracts and wants to do more testing. This one speck on sand could save your eyesight or even more, your life. We need to remember all the gifts that God gives us. At times, we may not know why, but we trust in the Lord, for there is a reason.

His splendor was like the sunrise; rays flashed from his hand, where his power was hidden.

(Habakkuk 3:4) NIV

ACTIONS SPEAK LOUDER THAN WORDS

We talk to our friends, coworkers and family on a daily basis. We talk about all kinds of subjects, including our beliefs in God. If we could not longer communicate by our mouth or hands and only by our actions, what type of person would we show others that we are? There is an old saying "talk the talk, but can you walk the walk?" This saying tells it all. We Christians can tell everyone that we have dedicated our life to Jesus Christ, however if our actions are not that of God's direction whom are we fooling? We are not fooling God! We are fooling others and ourselves into believing we are Christians. Our actions do speak louder than our words! God has given us all the resources that we need to talk the talk and walk the walk like a Christian. If at any point in our life that we feel we are only talking the talk or walking the walk of a Christian, we should stop right then, open our heart and soul up to God, and ask that He come into our lives. Ask Him for forgiveness and direction so that we can "talk the talk" and "walk the walk". We will be filled with the knowledge that we are doing the walking and talking of our Lord Jesus Christ.

They claim to know God, but by their actions they deny him. They are detestable, disobedient and unfit for doing anything good.

(Titus 1:16) NIV

ASHES IN THE FIRE

When we have a wood fire, the burnt wood leaves behind ashes. We know that life would not exist as we know it without some form of fire. We use fire for cooking, heating and many other uses. Christians also have a fire in them for the Lord's word. The fire of Our Lord consumes our heart and soul with love, faith, hope and salvation. Unlike ash that is the by-product of burnt wood, our by-product is the knowledge of knowing that we are doing the Lord's work. A wood fire must have wood added for the fire to continue. Christians also need to keep adding the word of God to their heart and soul so the fire remains strong within them. If we add wet or unseasoned wood to a fire, chances are the fire would go out because we added the wrong type of wood. This is also true with Christians; we could be led astray by following the words and actions of the unholy. Our fire for the Lord will start to fade as sin and corruption enters our heart and soul. We must always be on guard for the works of Satan; he would like to extinguish our fire that we have with our Lord. He would love to have another lost soul feeding his fire in hell. Stand strong on your Christian beliefs.

Therefore, since we are receiving a Kingdom that cannot be shaken, let us be thankful, and so worship God acceptably with reverence and awe, for our "God is a consuming fire."
(Hebrews 12:28-29) NIV

AVOIDING

Can you say that you never avoided anything? I do not think anyone can say that. God instructed us to avoid evil and sin. Some of us do a great job at this. Others are tempted all the time. This is where God comes to our rescue. Christians are not exempt from avoiding what is sinful and unholy; but we do have the tools and knowledge to avoid them. When we are ill with a cold, we go to a doctor. He gives us medicine to feel better. We do not avoid taking them. Christians sometimes avoid God, because they do not want help with their problems. They will ask non-qualified people for advice on how to handle their problems. These people can even quote the word of God, but remember what God has told us. He told us that others will come in His name, but they are not messengers of God. God does not want us fooled by their words. God has given us His teachers that are qualified here on earth for us to find the truth. The truth comes from reading God's word and from within our heart and soul. If we need help with a problem, do not avoid reading scripture and the advice given by qualified messengers of God.

To fear the lord is to hate evil; I hate pride and arrogance, evil behavior and perverse speech.

(Proverbs 8:13) NIV

Baby with a Bottle

Push, Push, just a little longer. This could be the first words you hear the day you were born. For the next few years you will depend on others for your food and safety. The older we get, the less we depend on others for our needs. We may feel life is going well and still feel something is missing. We decide to accept Jesus Christ as our Savior and become a Christian. This fills the void we are missing. We may try to lead the life of a Christian and feel going to church on Sunday keeps us strong in our beliefs. Wrong, God knows that we need to be nourished every day of the week with His words, and not only on Sunday to remain strong and healthy. He also knows that Christians will sin no matter what He gives us. This is why God has given us His gift of forgiveness. We may feel and act as adults but we remain as a small child in God's eyes. God will always be our father and care about us. His love is everlasting and He wants us to know that He is always there for us. Head to church on Sunday for your milk from God and don't forget about the rest of the week.

For we are taking pains to do what is right, not only in the eyes of the Lord but also in the eyes on men.

(2 Corinthians 8:21) NIV

Being Avoided

Many people will avoid true Christians that follow God's word. These can be family, friends, coworkers, strangers and even other Christians. They may not be invited to many parties because the host feels they would be offended by what could happen. People may be pre-warned about them, they may say things like "Did you know that he or she is big into religion?" They may also tell others to watch what they say around the true Christian because of their faith. True Christians also will be avoided by other Christians because of their self-guilt, they know that their actions are not that of a true follower of God and don't want the true Christians to see that. This action of others avoiding them is the best comment they can ever give a true Christian. This is telling a true Christian that they are with God's spirit and that others see what God has given them. True Christians are like a walking billboard, glowing with the Lord's Spirit. Their actions show others that they are bubbling over with the fruits of the Spirit and the true words of God.

> Do not be surprised, my brothers, if the world hates you. We know that we have passed from death to life, because we love our brothers. Anyone who does not love remains in death.
>
> (1 John 3:13 - 3:14) NIV

BETRAYED

We all feel betrayed at one point or another in our lifetime. This betrayal could come from a coworker, friend, or family member. Betrayal can come in the form of someone telling a lie to us or about us. When we are betrayed, we are hurt to some degree. Being betrayed will cause most of us to have ill feelings towards the person who betrayed us. Jesus Christ was betrayed many times. If the betrayer asked for forgiveness, we know the Lord would forgive them. We, on the other hand, have trouble forgiving people. We may say we forgive and believe it in our heart and soul. We, as Christians, must forgive unholy acts committed towards us. However, the trouble with our minds is that we retain a memory of the betrayal. This memory could cause us to hold this against the person that hurt us. We need to ask the Holy Spirit to come into our heart and soul to comfort us and help us not have ill feelings. We, as Christians, must remember that God gives His forgiveness for our actions.

If you argue your case with a neighbor, do not betray another man's confidence.

(Proverbs 25:9) NIV

Carrying Your Pail

God gave us His only son to die on the cross for our salvation. Jesus and His followers had to bear many hardships and even death preaching the Word of God. Jesus carried the whole pail knowing that He would give His life for our salvation. Throughout our life, we will make commitments to our jobs, family and friends that require us to carry our pail. God did not intend for us to carry the whole pail by ourselves, He wants us to share the weight of our duties. Christians sometime forget that when we make a commitment to marriage or friendships that we must share equally. If you think about trying to carry a full bucket of water up a hill, you can imagine putting all the weight to one side causing us to lean. If we shared the weight into two buckets, we would have equal weight on each side, allowing us to stand upright and making the journey easier. Christians must not be deceived in thinking that they can bear all the weight by themselves. It is very easy for a Christian to be fooled by thinking that they are doing the right thing by carrying the full weight trying to help others. God is the only one that bears the weight of all our sins and downfalls.

So that there should be no division in the body, but that its parts should have equal concern for each other.
(1 Corinthians 12:25) NIV

Cat Up the Tree

The cat is up the tree; its tail is all fluffed up. What happened? The cat was just playing in the yard, and a big dog started barking. The next thing you know, the cat is up the tree. The dog left the area and the cat is still in the tree and will not come down. Someone thinks they can climb the tree and help the cat down. When they reach out to help the cat, the cat scratches and bites them. They retreat down the tree saying, "Doesn't the cat know I'm just trying to help it?" Two days pass and the cat is still up the tree with no food or water. Sometime Christians act like this cat, something scares us and we run. Then someone tries to help us and we don't listen or want his or her help. Sometimes we are blinded by lies or beliefs that cause us to reject help from others. This is the time we must trust in God and His word. God's word will direct us, for it will not deceive or lie to us. The cat in time will come down from the tree, how it comes down is the question. It could fall out of the tree because it becomes too weak to hold on or climb down and return to the safety of its home. When we have a problem or need help in our life, turn to God, for He will not lead us astray!

God is our refuge and strength, an ever-present help in trouble.
(Psalm 46:1) NIV

Changes of Lifestyle

We all have changes in our life—some good and some bad. Christians that accept Jesus Christ as their savior have major changes in their lifestyle! They view the whole world and their actions with a new set of eyes and ears; their whole life is turned around with the power of the Holy Spirit. They will feel the changes within their heart and soul. They will feel God's love and direction all the time. Their mission in life will be that of God's and not themselves. Their friends, family and acquaintances will also see and hear the changes. Their views as a Christian will cause some of their friends, family and acquaintances to space themselves from them. The main reason for this is they fear the truth of the Lord. There will also be some so-called Christians that will space themselves because of the fear they will be discovered as fake believers. These people read what they want into God's word to suit their needs or make excuses for their actions.

Jesus said to the woman, "Your faith has saved you; go in peace."

(Luke 7:50) NIV

Choices

We all go through our life making choices. We will have small choices; like what clothes to wear, what foods to eat, etc. These choices will have small impacts on our life. We will also have choices that will have a greater impact—like buying a car, a house, or other things that will have a long-term effect on our life. Then there are the lifelong choices we make that influence our life and others forever, including our salvation. Some, but not all, of our choices that we make could be our faith in the Lord Jesus Christ, marriage, having children, and how we conduct our lives. God has given man the power to make his own choices in life. God will help us, if we ask. When we make choices, we must insure that it is a choice from God and not a choice of the flesh. We may feel like we have made wrong choices, but this is where God and the Holy Spirit are needed. We do not want to compound our mistakes by thinking we do not need God's help. If we attempt to do this, we are taking our life and salvation into our own hands and this is not what God wants. We can run from ourselves, but where are we going? We can say we know this is right, but what is right? We can say that it is for the best, but what is best? We can say everyone is doing it, but what is it? We can say we will be better off, but what is better off? We can say they will be better off, but who are they? We can say we will feel better, but what is better? The old saying is "the grass is greener on the other side of the fence." We must remember that it is not the grass, but the seed that produces the grass that counts.

The same goes for everything we do in our life -- we will reap what we sow. If we only put the negatives into something, our decisions and choices will relate to this thinking. We, as Christians, need to seek the Lord's help and not that of the flesh! May God forgive us should we fail to follow His words.

> If anyone chooses to do God's will, he will find out whether my teaching comes from God or whether I speak on my own.
>
> (John 7:17) NIV

CLOUDS IN THE SKY

We can go outside on a sunny day and not find a cloud in the sky. We can feel all the rays of the sun throughout our body, and it feels great. We can go outside on a different day and only see a small glimmer of the sun peaking through the clouds; we don't get the same feeling we have on sunny days. God's rays are shining for us each and every day of our life. We may encounter some days when situations or problems in our life may cause a fog to block some of God's rays, but not all of them. God is ready and willing to help clear up the fog. Sometimes we try to play God and think that we could drink or take drugs to self-medicate ourselves while we wait for God's help. Wrong! What makes you think you can hear what God is telling you when you don't know what you're telling yourself? God does not what any of His children lost in the fog, He wants to help us, but we must first help ourselves. We can tell ourselves that this is because of all the pressure we are under and once the problems are over we'll stop. Quit lying to yourself and others! Most of all, quit lying to God, He is not a fool! You will find some other lame excuse. If we find ourselves in the company of family or friends that support your actions, they also need guidance from God. We need fellow Christians to help us through these hard times and most of all we need to put our trust in God, not a bottle or drugs.

> As a shepherd looks after his scattered flock when he is with them,
> so will I look after my sheep. I will rescue them from all the places
> where they were scattered on a day of clouds and darkness.
>
> (Ezekiel 34:12) NIV

CONFUSION

What is confusion? We all have our own beliefs about what causes confusion. We as Christians know that the Lord has told us Satan is the controller of confusion. Gods gave us His words in the Bible where He spelled out how we should worship Him. He also has instructed us how to carry out our lives through Him. We will have times when confusion enters our life, this is the time we as Christians must find the strength and courage to reject these unholy thoughts. Satan will make us believe that these unholy thoughts are from God. This could cause us to take the wrong course of action. God knows that Satan has this power over us. God gives us the Holy Spirit to show us clear thoughts so we can know right from wrong. If you should ever find yourself confused over something, re-member this is the work of Satan.

Immediately the boy's father exclaimed, "I do believe; help me to overcome my unbelief!"

(Mark 9:24) NIV

DAMNATION

23

Christians should not fear this word. Damnation is a place no one ever wants to be headed. We have an obligation to spread the Gospel to our friends, coworkers, and anyone in need of His Word. When a sinner is committed to condemnation, he or she will suffer everlasting punishment with no relief ever! We do not become a sinner overnight. We are born sinners and we must decide if we are going to accept God as our savior, so that we can have salvation in the Lord's home. People who choose not to accept God as their savior and continue to have fun, enjoying the sins of the flesh for the short time here on earth, can look forward to having all of eternity to enjoy Satan's comforts of hell. May we pray that all lost souls find the Word of God, our Savior, and accept Jesus Christ into their soul so that they can have everlasting salvation with God.

For the evil man has no future hope, and the lamp of the wicked will be snuffed out.

(Proverbs 24:20) NIV

Do as I say, but not as I do

Translation "HYPOCRITE"

One who affects virtues or qualities he or she does not have. We all experience times when we are called upon to help a person in need. This could be a loved one, friend or a total stranger. It would be very wise for us to examine our ability to help this person. We, as Christians, sometimes feel the need to help without the knowledge and experience to help.

We ask the person to please….Stop drinking so much, because you always get drunk.But we can have a drink, because we know when to stop.

Do not smoke, because it is not good for you.But we smoke very few cigarettes, but not a pack a day.

Don't go to the bar and drink with your friends, because you could come home drunk.

But we go to the bar with our friends and drink just to relax.

Don't steal things, because you'll get in trouble. But we say we only borrow things and forget to return them and that's not stealing.

Don't hang around those types of friends, because they all drink and do drugs. But we hang with friends that do the same thing.

Don't do crack or other drugs; they are bad for you. But we smoke pot; it's not a hard drug.

Don't speed in the car.But it's all right for us to speed, because we need to get there in a hurry.

Don't use foul language. But we use foul language, but we only do it when we are mad.

Christians must lead by example. We know what God's Word expects of us.

"Why do you look at the speck of sawdust in your brother's eye and pay no attention to the plank in your own eye? How can you say to your brother, 'Let me take the speck out of your eye,' when all the time there is a plank in your own eye? You hypocrite, first take the plank out of your own eye, and then you will see clearly to remove the speck from your brother's eye.

(Matthew 7:3 - 7:5) NIV

Don't I Look Great!

What is the first thought that comes to your mind when you hear someone say "Don't I look great?" Conceited, self-centered? There are people in this world that only think of themselves first and everybody else second. They feel and think that they should be the center of attention. There are Christians that act this way. They present themselves to others as knowledgeable with the Word of God and can quote Bible verses. They feel qualified to advise others in God's Word and in what God wants. They can tell you what you want to hear by reading into His word what they want to hear. Do not be fooled by this type of Christian, God has warned us about false prophets (Matthew 7:15). God is to be first in our life. The only one that knows what God wants is God. We have the Bible to instruct us on what God requires of us. God does not want any Christian to jump up and down yelling, "Look at me, look what I know." Christians are not on an island by themselves or in a cult preaching the word of God their way. God wants Christians to fellowship with other Christians, which is accomplished by going to church. Therefore, the big question is: How do we deal with self-centered people? One way is asking them if they read Matthew 23.

In the same way, on the outside you appear to people as righteous, but on the inside you are full of hypocrisy and wickedness.

(Matthew 23:28) NIV

FAMILY

God's greatest creation is that of man and woman. We should thank Him every day for the gift of having a family. The family is the core of life. Without the family, we are nothing. One of God's best works is that of a Christian family that praises Him. Satan will do whatever he can to stop God's family from succeeding. If God's family fails, it is not only a failure to man but also an embarrassment to God. We may find ourselves unhappy in our family at times, but this is the work of Satan, not God. God wants us to be happy in our family and wants us to take action so that our families succeed. We are given the Holy Spirit and the Word of God to assist us in maintaining a strong Christian family.

If anyone dos not provide for his relatives, and especially for his immediate family, he has denied the faith and is worse than an unbeliever.

(1 Timothy 5:8) NIV

FEEDING

Have you ever been told you are going to turn into what you eat? People eat foods that are good for their body to feel healthy. Some people only drink natural juices or water to stay healthy. Some people eat anything they want without caring about their body. The body has many ways or telling us if we are not doing something right. When a person feels they are overweight, or out of shape they will try to eat healthier foods and exercise to look or feel better. Christians also need to feed on God's word to enrich their heart and soul. We can receive some of our feeding by reading the Bible, going to God's house, and praying. Like our body, we can also hurt our heart and soul by feeding on unholy thoughts or actions. Christians must not forget that they have given their heart and soul to God. Sometimes we feed our heart and soul with unhealthy actions and thoughts that start to erode the good and replace it with… If we ever question what to feed on, think first, if Jesus were with us, would we still do it? If not, why are we doing it? To satisfy the wants of the flesh? By the way, He is with us all the time! Go out right now and have a feeding on God's Word, you will feel better.

Yet the Lord longs to be gracious to you; he rises to show you compassion. For the Lord is a God of justice. Blessed are all who wait for him!

(Isaiah 30:18) NIV

FISHING WITHOUT …?

Let's go fishing. We are all set. We have the boat all hooked up, we have packed our lunch, we have placed all the gear in the boat, we have the bait, and the weather is great. Now, we are sitting in our boat located right over our favorite fishing hole. The fish finder shows more fish then we ever seen before just under the boat. We get our pole ready, reach for the bait and then we notice we do not have any hooks. Christians go out into the world thinking that they also have all the equipment needed. We must not believe that just because we always do it that we could not forget something. As the fisherman, we could get complacent and this could cause us to be unprepared. God has given us the equipment to be prepared, but sometimes we feel we do not need it. This is a very bad mistake on our part. We have His words in the Bible, His church to fellowship in and the Holy Spirit to guide us; along with everything else He has given us. These are given to us to use to be prepared as Christians. Let us not be like the fisherman without any hooks. The fisherman saw a friend on the lake and borrowed some hooks. We call this fellow hook sharing.

Preach the word; be prepared in season and out of season; correct, rebuke and encourage with great patience and careful instruction.

(2 Timothy 4:2) NIV

Flying in the Clouds

Why are you not happy? You are free as bird in the sky flying high above all your problems; you asked to be set free. You have been granted freedom by your own accord, but you do not seem happy. You have been released from your cage that was surrounding you, now you have all the sky to travel, as you wanted. You are now free to do all the things you dreamed about without restrictions, you are in control, you are your own master, and you answer to no one but yourself. Our own thoughts and others sometime misguide us into thinking that our current situation is wrong and that there is a better way of living. We pray to God to help us and show us the way, but sometimes we hear what He tells us and we still do not listen. We take actions on our own that are contrary to the wishes of God's and for a short time we may feel justified in our actions. This could cause us to feel unhappy when we have total freedom as we wanted, because we acted without the God's Spirit and acted on our own. We must remember that there are evil forces all around us trying to separate us from the Lord. Do not be led astray by the word of Satan and his spirits.

Dear friends, do not believe every spirit, but test the spirits to see whether they are from God, because many false prophets have gone out into the world.

(1 John 4:1) NIV

FOCUS

When God created man, He gave us great gifts pertaining to our bodies. One of those gifts is our eyesight. We can see things far off in the distance or things right up to our nose. We can view all the wonders of God just by opening our eyes. With this gift, we can go through life looking at a wide screen view or narrow view. We have to choose how we are going to look at life. We can focus on the problems we are having or put the problems in perspective and look at the whole picture. If we bang our toe into something and it hurts badly, we focus only on the hurt toe and not the other parts of the body that are fine. Think about a basket of oranges— if we see only one orange rotten, would we throw the whole basket out? We can face problems every day at work, at home, and with friends or our loved ones. We sometime focus only at the problem area and do not see the whole picture, we may view our problem as not fixable and want to throw the whole thing out. If God had this viewpoint, we would have no chance of salvation. God has the wide screen view of His children and does not focus only on the rotten; He gave us His only son Jesus Christ to let us know that. When we encounter a problem in our life, we need to look at the whole picture and not focus only on the problems. This may seem impossible for us to do at times, but with God's help and our prayers, He will show us the way. Let's not throw the whole basket of oranges out because of one of them being rotten, make orange juice with the bad one.

For physical training is of some value, but godliness has value for all things, holding promise for both the present life and the life to come.

(1 Timothy 4:8) NIV

FREE TRIAL OFFER

Free trial offers are a common sales ploy used by all types of businesses. We can get them in the mail, read about the offers in the newspaper and magazines, see them on the television and even receive phone calls. They all want us to buy some type of service or product, and tell us if we do not want the service or product after an established amount of time all we have to do is call and cancel or just return the product. They even tell us no hassles or questions if we return or cancel them. Their thinking in this type of offer is that we will forget about the amount of time that was established for us to return or cancel. Think about this, we get something for what we feel is free. Then when the time is up, they will then start billing us. Satan also uses this type of ploy, he wants us to sin and forget about it and we keep sinning. Before long, we end up paying the highest price ever. Christians know that it is easy to fall in to the sinning mode, which is why we must remain strong with our Lord. Free trial offers can also be good if we are in the market for the product or service. Being pressured or doing something we do not want is wrong. Remember if we are ever pressured into doing anything that feels wrong, do not do it! God will be there to support us.

> We do not want you to be uninformed, brothers, about the hardships we suffered in the province of Asia. We were under great pressure, far beyond our ability to endure, so that we despaired even in life.
>
> (2 Corinthians 1:8) NIV

Good day My Child

I have given you this day to enjoy.

Be thankful for all My gifts.

I will be with you all day and night.

Do not let the evil one enter your mind or thoughts.

I love you and have forgiven all your sins.

Be thankful for your family, for they love and respect you.

Give Me all your burdens.

For My will, will be done.

Have faith in Me with your heart and soul.

When you feel down, call upon Me.

I will not lead you astray.

The Lord is far from the wicked but he hears the prayers of the righteous.

(Proverbs 15:29) NIV

Grab That Brass Ring

Have you ever heard the saying, "If only I could grab that brass ring?" Some people go through life thinking they always come up short. There are many people that will come up short, but it may not be while they occupy the body they have now. Our life here on earth is only a short piece of time compared to eternity. Christians will never come up short when it comes to everlasting life with Jesus Christ. With God as our strength and provider, we can go through life knowing we have the brass ring in our hand. Believing in God will not stop us from encountering problems just like every one else. We will encounter situations and difficulty just by being part of the human race. By believing in God and having salvation, we do make choices based on God's words. Christians are not exempt from making bad choices in life. Being a Christian gives us the opportunity to ask for forgiveness and guidance so as not to make the same mistake again.

What if he did this to make the riches of his glory known to the objects of his mercy, whom he prepared in advance for glory.

(Romans 9:23) NIV

HAPPINESS

35

We always want to be happy in our life. God also wants us to be happy. We sometimes question if we are really happy. We can have every material thing on earth handed to us, but are we truly happy? Probably not. The only true way to find happiness is through our Lord God. He has given us so many things that sometimes we don't see them all. We may have happiness right in front of us and not feel that way. This is how Satan wants us to feel. He will attempt to confuse us and cause us to be unhappy. Satan will put thoughts into our minds and hearts telling us we were not happy. He will block all the love and good things and only show us the things that make us unhappy. This is Satan's way of destroying what God has given to us. If you are unhappy, ask the Holy Spirit to come into you and show you the way. This is God's way. Christians are a target for Satan; so be alert to corrupt thoughts of the mind and body.

A happy heart makes the face cheerful, but the heartache crushes the spirit.

(Proverbs 15:13) NIV

Help! I'm Stuck

If you heard someone yelling for help, you would see if you could help him or her. If you had the power or knowledge to help, you would. This is the role God has given Christians, to help their fellow neighbors and friends. Christians sometimes think they can help a friend or neighbor with their problems, while in reality, they could be having the same problems, but they are incapable of helping themselves. If we do help and are not trained or knowledgeable in what we should or should not say or do, we could cause a small problem to escalate into a major problem. Sometimes we forget our limitations as a Christian, and we think with God on our side we can help everyone. God has given each of us special gifts and one of those gifts may not be counseling others. We can best help our family or friends by directing them to fellow Christians who are trained to assist them. We can support them with prayers. Please pray that we are not deceived about what we can and cannot do! Remember that God has given each of us our own special gifts!

David went out to meet them and said to them, "If you have come to me in peace, to help me, I am ready to have you unite with me. But if you have come to betray me to my enemies when my hands are free from violence, may the God of our fathers see it and judge you."

(1 Chronicles 12:17) NIV

How Dare You

How dare you use the Word of God for your own gain and satisfaction? The Word of God is just that, God's Word, not yours. God has made it very clear what is demanded of His followers. If you think for one second that He wants you to interpret His Words to meet your needs or wants, you're wrong. The Bible has a very clear and defined meaning. Christians must not allow themselves to fall into Satan's grip. If you even think that you are not in accordance with God's wishes, the likelihood is that you are acting in the evil one's ways. If you have the seed of the Lord planted within your heart and soul, then act that way! Many Christians have fallen into sin because of questioning the Lord. Christians that fall into sin blame everyone else for their problems and situations, saying God is testing them. They try to find the answers without God's help or direction. They rely on themselves or others for direction. The tragedy of these actions is that they keep falling farther and farther away from what God wants or demands. They start believing that what they are doing is God's wishes and in reality, they are doing Satan's wishes. God wants his Words followed and that we be happy and enjoy a fruitful life with Him. Satan, on the other hand, will stop at nothing to destroy what is good in life. He will use his version of God's Word to work for his goals and not that of the Lord's.

Their visions are false and their divinations a lie. They say, "The LORD declares," when the LORD has not sent them; yet they expect their words to be fulfilled.

(Ezekiel 13:6) NIV

How Do You Feel?

"How do you feel" is a question people may ask you many times. The response you give may say a lot about yourself. People may respond in a positive way by saying "fantastic, great, good, and not bad at all." The negative type responses may be like "I'm making it, as well as expected, things could be better," and "all right I guess." Christians have been given the gift of everlasting life with the Lord; they have the knowledge that heaven awaits them, so most of the time they are feeling on top of the world. The feelings we have both physically and emotionally can be caused by our actions and the way we think. If we eat something and later we feel ill we know it could have been the food, if we pick up something hot and we burn our hand we know it's because of what we picked up. Christians also can get an ill feeling by thinking or acting inappropriately. If we know that we are doing something wrong we can cause ourselves to become ill. The Holy Spirit can also cause us to feel uneasy because of our actions; this may be a message for us to clean up our act. So how do you feel?

Like the blind we grope along the wall, feeling our way like men without eyes. At midday we stumble as if it were twilight; among the strong, we are like the dead.

(Isaiah 59:10) NIV

I Can Not Recall

Our lives are full of daily tasks. Our minds are always working, we are always on the go, doing this or that and by the end of the day we may ask ourselves where did the time go? We sometime do things so often they become routine. We get up pray, make the bed, brush our teeth, comb our hair, make toast, drive to work, come home, eat supper, go to bed etc.; in between all this there are many, many things happening we probably do not recall doing. Did we tell our loved ones that we love them, say goodbye, tell our friends good morning, and thank God for all He has done for us? This is routine, routine, routine! How can we enjoy all the gifts God has given us if we just go through the motions of living? We need to be aware of what we are doing at all times and not just go through the motions. We were not created as robots. God created us in His image. We should pray and share our daily tasks and thoughts with Him, and not only on Sundays. He wants to be with us all of the time, hearing us and directing us, he wants us to confide in Him. The only reason we have what we have is because of His grace. We may forget that He is in control, not us! Think about this, If He is not with us all the time who do you think will be there? Satan? We must never forget who is the boss is, it's not us!

"And when you pray, do not keep babbling like pagans, for they think they will be heard because of their many words. Do not be like them, for your Father knows what you need before you ask him."

(Matthew 6:7 & 6:8) NIV

I Can Not See It

Many Christians go through life believing in God, even if they cannot see or hear Him. The truth is that we do see and hear Him every day of our life. He gives us everything we have and need to survive. He gives us His love along with the love of our families. We sometimes see this in black and white without seeing all the wonderful colors He has given us. God did intend for us to be happy with all His gifts, but we sometimes fail to see these gifts because we are distracted by Satan's traps. We concentrate on what is wrong and not all that good, we become obsessed with the bad. The bad starts to eat away the truth a little bit at a time until this is all we concentrate on. Our Spirit is strong with God's Word but or bodies become weak and this causes us to act on our own. This is where we need to allow the Holy Spirit to take control and lead us out of Satan's hold! We can continue in the direction that Satan has planned for us or we can follow God's direction. If we do, it is our choice. We know right from wrong if the seed of God is planted deep within our heart and soul. If we need to see God, look to the heavens and read His word. This is His direction to happiness and salvation. Have unyielding faith in God's Word!

Whatever happens, conduct yourselves in a manner worthy of the gospel of Christ. Then, whether I come and see you in my absence, I will know that you stand firm in one spirit, contending as one man for the faith of the gospel.

(Philippians 1:27) NIV

I Didn't Know That

Did you know that God gave us his only son to die on the cross for your salvation? Did you know that Jesus Christ was God's only son? Did you know that the Bible was written for us? Did you know that God would forgive your sins? Did you know that Satan is the master of confusion? Did you know God wants you to spread His word? Did you know that God wants you to fellowship with others? Did you know that God loves you? Did you know that Jesus rose from the dead? Did you know that accepting and believing in Jesus Christ you have salvation? Did you know that Satan is evil? Did you know God is always with you? Did you know that God gave us the Holy Spirit? Did you know Satan wants to destroy all Gods gifts He has given you? Did you know God would never leave you nor forsake you?

If you know all this, why would you ever want anything other than what God has promised? We sometimes forget all the wonderful gifts God has given us, and we question why we do not get what we want. We must remember that God is the giver of everlasting life. We sometimes need a wake up call to realize all we have, and what little we could have without God in our life. Think about that!

Great are the works of the Lord; they are pondered by all who delight in them. Glorious and majestic are his deeds, and his righteousness endures forever.

(Psalm 111:2 & 111:3) NIV

I Give Up

I tried and failed. I no longer can go on with this battle. I am only made of flesh and blood. I cannot take on the deeds and wishes of Satan in my life. I tried and failed. I prayed to God to show me the way. I have the power of salvation through our Lord Jesus. It is there for the asking. I have the power of the Holy Spirit within me to see the truth. I cannot force myself to see the truth. I have tried to see His way, but I avoided His truths. I know God and His Word. I know His powers. I know what is right and what is wrong. Only I can ask for salvation to save myself. I will pray that I find the truth, but I cannot fight the battle. May God have mercy on my soul for failing without seeking God's help. May He come to me and save me from evil.

"Have faith in God," Jesus answered.

(Mark 11:22) NIV

I Lost that Feeling

43

We may sometimes feel lost in life and don't know where to go. We may have heard that God is available to everyone on earth just for the asking, but we may feel we have been too bad in our life for anyone to forgive us. This may be true for man to forgive us, but it is not true for God to forgive us. God will forgive us for any sins that we have committed in the past, no matter what. When we accept Jesus Christ as our savior and that He died on the cross for our sins, at that second all of our sins have been forgiven. We will then be graced with the power of the Holy Spirit and all the gifts God has to offer. We must follow the words written in the Bible to maintain a healthy relationship with God. We will be graced with being a Christian and joining the family of God. We will be able to walk with the fruit of the Spirit in our heart and soul.

"Is not my house right with God? Has he not made with me an everlasting covenant, arranged and secured in every part? Will he not bring to fruition my salvation and grant me my every desire?

(2 Samuel 23:5)NIV

In Charge

We want to be the boss, leader, decision maker, and controller. We want to be in charge and want the say-so on what goes on in our life. We don't want people to tell us what we can or cannot do. As Christians, we are to turn over all control of our life to God. The problem is that we are only human and sometimes forget that the Lord is in control. When we start to have problems in our life we sometimes forget who the boss is, try to figure out what the problem is, and take actions to resolve them ourselves. We may get lucky and resolve the problem but in most cases they get worst or the problem is still there and we just don't see it. Satan has a way of corrupting our thinking when things start to go wrong within our life. His goal is to make us think we can handle the problem without Gods assistance. We must trust God with all of our decisions no matter how small they are. He will allow the Holy Spirit to guide us in the right direction. Let us not forget whom the boss, leader, decision maker, controller is! God our Father is in charge.

"Commit to the Lord whatever you do, and your plans will succeed."

(Proverbs 16:3) NIV

It is All in the Timing

Have you ever watched a baseball game and wondered how the batter hits a ball coming at him around 100 miles per hour? It's all done with mirrors. That's not true. It comes with many years of practice, timing the swing of the bat to meet the ball when it crosses over the plate. To be a productive member of the human race and a Christian, we need to operate in life using some form of established time. Some may say they are doing their own thing and do not live by man's time. Surprise! God did not intend for us to live in our own little world. He intended for us to live life with our fellow brothers and sisters in fellowship. God has many gifts for us throughout our lifetime, but it will come in God's timing. When we experience situations in our life when it seems everything is going wrong, we need to trust in the Lord. He will guide and comfort us through our time of need. We need to be patience because God works in His time, not ours. We should not try to wonder what God wants us to do; He will guide us with His Spirit. Satan is the master of confusion, not our Lord! When Sunday comes, don't forget what time God's service starts at church!

Sow for yourselves righteousness, reap the fruit of the unfailing love, and break up your unplowed ground; for it is time to seek the Lord, until he comes and showers righteousness on you.

(Hosea 10:12) NIV

JUDGING

We are instructed by God not to judge others. God did say we should judge ourselves. We, as Christians, must always look at our actions. We are not above having sinful thoughts or committing unholy acts. We need to be on guard from Satan and his followers at all times. We sometimes do things that seem "OKAY" and we feel that there is no harm in it. This stems from what is acceptable in today's culture. The Bible does not say we do not have to follow His word about some sins, because everyone is doing it and it is acceptable. The Bible was written for our salvation and its definition of sin is very clear. We can be led into sin because it feels good and right at the time. Well if sin hurts us, do you think we would do it? No, we would not! This is why sin is so easy to do. It feels good and that's exactly what Satan wants. If life would be without thorns from sin, we would not need to work at keeping our guard up because everything would feel right. This would be living without rights and wrongs. As Christians, we must accept God as our only way to salvation. Judge yourself by the actions you take or thoughts you have. Are they of God or are they of Satan? If you have any trouble with your response, step back and take note! If you are following God's word, you will not have any questions as to your actions or thoughts. God does not give us confusion; that's the work of Satan. We, as Christians, make a lifelong commitment to follow His Word, not only when it suits us. Judge yourself as God would judge you, because He will!

For the Word of God is living and active. Sharper than any double-edged sword, it penetrates even to dividing soul and spirit, joints and marrow; it judges the thoughts and attitudes of the heart.

(Hebrews 4:12) NIV

JUST PASSING THROUGH

Most of us pick the location were we want to live and raise our family. Sometimes we have to live in the area were we work. This may not be the area that you would have chosen to raise your family; however, you cannot choose your job location. We may think and plan that if the opportunity presents itself, we will move to a better job or location. We could think that we are only at this location until we can move, so we feel we are only passing though and try not to put down roots. Our life here on earth is only a temporary location for our soul. We are only passing though until our death. Our soul can only go to one of two places, Heaven or Hell. We have to choose where we want to go. God has given us the path and direction for us to find everlasting salvation with Him in Heaven. It does not matter where we are living; it's how we are living. The question we must ask ourselves is "have we accepted Jesus Christ as our Savior?" If we have, then we know that God wants us to share His word with others anywhere we live. Remember that our life now is only a stepping-stone to Heaven, we are just passing through. Let our life represent that of a Christian so that we can assure the next location of our soul.

So the Twelve gathered all disciples together and said, "It would not be right for us to neglect the ministry of the Word of God in order to wait on tables."

(Acts 6:2) NIV

JUSTIFYING

49

Do not use My Words to deceive yourself or others to suit your situation or to justify your actions, for they are not My Words. They are your words and thoughts. My Words are that of rightfulness and not of excuses. I have given you the Holy Bible to follow. I speak the word of truth and salvation. The truth of My Word will set you free from the thoughts and actions of the evil one within you. Open your heart and soul so that I can enter for I long to be with you. Do not confuse My Word for that of the evil one. Listen to My messengers for they have My Word within them, for they will not mislead you. Awake from the darkness of the evil one and follow My light, for I am the truth and salvation. Believe in me with all your heart and the thoughts of the evil one will flee from you.

We live by faith, not by sight.

(2 Corinthians 5:7) NIV

Keep On Running

Our life is full of doing things with our families, friends, and working or playing just to name a few. We may set aside an hour or two for church a week but that all the time we have available. We sometimes feel time flies by before we ever get a chance to rest; we have schedules to meet and appointments to keep. The major things that must be done we insure that we set aside time to take care of them, people are counting on us and we don't want to disappoint them. We sometimes put others in front of ourselves to the point we no longer have control and we feel overwhelmed. We are at a point where we really don't know what we want because we are no longer in control. One of the reasons that we may feel this way is because we have not kept God first; we put others and ourselves in that position. This is the time we need to stop, re-examine ourselves and put God first in our lives. This will allow Him to comfort us and direct us in His direction without having outside influences. Satan loves it when we are concerned more about pleasing others and ourselves before the Lord, because he knows he can take control easier without God in our life.

You were running a good race. Who cut in on you and kept you from obeying the truth? That kind of persuasion does not come from the one who calls you. "A little yeast works through the whole batch of dough." I am confident in the Lord that you will take no other view. The one who is throwing you into confusion will pay the penalty, whoever he may be.

(Galatians 5:7 – 5:10) NIV

LIFE'S SITUATIONS

51

Unforeseen and general problems that we encounter in life can drain the Spirit from our body like the air out of a tire. This can cause us to feel as if we are going through the motions of living without really living. This is the time Satan will attack us with all his might, causing us confusion and unrest. He will use any means possible to maintain his will over us. This is the time God wants us to lie down in green pastures with Him so that He can restore His Word and Spirit in us. We must, as children of God, welcome Him in our lives and follow the writing of His words. We must keep faith in Our Lord for He will not forsake us.

I love those who love me and those who seek me find me.
(Proverbs 8:17) NIV

LIMITS

We are given all types of limits. There are limits on alcohol consumption, speed limits as well as many other limits placed on us. Disregarding these limits can cause problems and unrest in our life. The law of the land can place these limits on us, but the most important are God's limits. God tells us that He wants us to be happy on this earth and wants us to enjoy the fruits He has given us. He gives us clear directions of what limits He wants us to follow. God's limits are written in the Bible. We, being of flesh and blood, can and sometimes will push these limits. This is when we must stop and ask forgiveness for our actions. We must also ask for His strength and fortitude to stop committing them. We can come up with many reasons for exceeding the set limits, but the real reason is that we want to. If we are true to our God, we need to take responsibility for our actions and not blame others for the things we do. We, not someone else, control our thoughts and actions. Others can influence us, but we do it. We should know what is written in the Bible and know right from wrong. The Bible was not given to us to be a dust collector or a book taking up space. You may not like the results of disobeying the limits of the Lord!

Nor thieves nor the greedy nor drunkards nor slanderers nor swindlers will inherit the Kingdom of God.

(1 Corinthians 6:10) NIV

LONELY

53

We all feel lonely from time to time. Someone could be in a room full of people and still feel lonely. Christians are never alone when they believe in the Lord Jesus Christ and His word. Non-Christians can have friends of the flesh and never feel lonely, but in God's eyes, they are alone. Non-Christians sometimes feel lost and insecure about themselves without knowing why. In some cases, they will do things to feel wanted or try to feel in control. We can see this all around us in the crimes people commit or the type of sinful employment they have. Christians must always be on guard to protect their belief in God and His word. This will assure that if we ever do feel alone all we need to do is pray and the Holy Spirit will be with us. Christians need to pray that all people without the knowledge and acceptance of the Lord Jesus Christ can find the truth.

> Let me live that I may praise you, and may your laws sustain me. I have strayed like a lost sheep. Seek your servant, for I have not forgotten your commands.
>
> (Psalm 119:175, 176) NIV

LOOK WHAT I FOUND

Think about going shopping at the mall or a sporting goods store for the whole day. You looked at all the things you wanted to. You may have picked up a few things you needed or just wanted. You are having a great day and nothing seems to be going wrong. As you're walking, you see a small paper bag lying out in the parking lot, so you check it out and find it full of money. You look around to see if anyone is looking for it, then you check and see if there is any identification that would tell you whom it belongs to. You find none. Being a good Christian, you inform the police and maybe the store office that you found something and if someone reports losing something to let you know. Well, for us to find something, someone had to lose it. God gave us His only son Jesus Christ for us to find salvation and everlasting life with Him. Jesus had to lose His life for us to gain salvation. We can find salvation by following God's words along with the words Jesus spoke during His short time on earth in our Bible. The next time you find something, think about what you found while having the Lord with you. What do you think happened with the bag of money?

And when she finds it, she calls her friends and neighbors together and says, "Rejoice with me; I have found my lost coin."

(Luke 15:9) NIV

Lord Please Help Me Too

Think of my words before I speak.
Think of others before I act.
Listen to what others are saying.
Be compassionate of others.
Know when to speak and not speak.
Be thankful for what I have.
Remember the gifts You have given me.
Not to be envious of others.
Give thanks and prayer to You each day.
Forgive others as You forgave me.
Remember that You are always there for me.
Share the Word of God with others.
Remember that I have given my life to You.
Give You all my burdens.
Love You with all my heart and soul.

Yet I am poor and needy; may the Lord think of me. You are
my help and my deliverer; O my God, do not delay.

(Psalm 40:17) NIV

Love You

The words of God to mankind say - He loves you. If it were not for the love of God, we would not have the opportunity for salvation and everlasting life with God. God's love for us is unyielding! He gave us His only son to die on the cross for our sins because He loves us! When we accept Jesus Christ as our savior, we are telling God our love for Him is also unyielding. Throughout life, we will use these two words to different degrees. We can say we love fishing, steak, football, etc. Are we willing to sacrifice everything for these things? When God grants us a spouse and a family, and when we tell them we love them, are we willing to sacrifice everything for them as God sacrificed Jesus for us? Our love is to be unconditional to our spouse and family as it is written in the Bible. We can read throughout the Bible were it is written that God loves us. We must not ever forget what God has sacrificed so that we can have salvation!

How long, O men, will you turn my glory to shame? How long will you love delusions and seek false gods? Know that the Lord has set apart the godly for himself; the Lord will hear when I call to him.

(Psalm 4:2 - 4:3) NIV

MAKE IT QUICK

In today's culture, we expect quick satisfaction! Some Christians go to church on Sunday expecting the service to last one hour and if it runs over, they get upset. Why cook when we can go out to eat? Why clean the house or car if it will only get dirty again? Why build a house, when we can just go buy one that is completely finished? Why bake a cake when we can just run to the store and buy one? Why work on a marriage when if we are unhappy; we can just divorce? Why work hard at a job? If we do not like it, we can get another one. Why wait for God to answer our prayers? We feel that we can fix the problem now. The quick satisfaction is what some people want and they don't want to waste their time on anything. For example, we don't want to make dinner at night because it takes time to prepare the food, cook it, set the table, eat and clean it all up. Christians must grow and mature with the Spirit of God's Word. God wants us to realize that everything that matters takes time to get better; He does not want us to think there is a quick fix to anything. God sets the time frame on answering our prayers, not us.

Then I realized that it is good and proper for a man to eat and drink, and to find satisfaction in his toilsome labor under the sun during the few days of life God has given him - for this is his lot.

(Ecclesiastes 5:18) NIV

MASQUERADING

Have you ever heard the saying "a wolf in sheep's clothing?" This is one saying to remember. We will talk to many people that say they are followers of Christ. We must take the warning God has given us when He told us many would come in His name, claiming to be followers, but they are not what they say. They will know the Word of God and all His requirements of Christians. This is the problem with people masquerading as fellow Christians. The person that masquerades as a Christian is one of the most deadly of people you will ever meet. This person will turn the Word of God around to meet their wants, needs, and desires. This person can also fool Christians easily. If we ever have questions, we should read the word of God. We, as Christians, must follow the word of God and not read into it what we want to hear. People that are masquerading as Christians may not know that they are working for Satan. They will feel that God is controlling their actions but in reality, Satan is. Remember that if it seems ungodly, then it is. Do not be fooled by a masquerading Christian for this may endanger your salvation with our Lord. Let God control your life and actions. A true Christian knows what is right in the eyes of God.

And no wonder, for Satan himself masquerades as an angel of light.

(2 Corinthians 11:14) NIV

ON THE RUN

You are fighting the battle and you do not know if you can keep going. You been fighting this battle for many years praying to God to help you and comfort you. God sends you help, but you start to retreat instead of standing and fighting. You retreat to the safety of … ? The battle seems less important now that you retreated, you have not given up but now you only fight when you want to. The help that was sent to you to win the battle, you abandoned. You still attempt to fight the battle only when you need to. You are happy at your safe haven and feel you are winning. God has answered your prayers with the help you need to win, but the evil one has persuaded you to retreat. The evil one knows that the longer time you are away from the battle the less you will fight. The evil one has compromised your battle plans and you do not see it. The enemy has infiltrated your headquarters and led you to total failure. Christians sometimes give up when God sends them help to win their battles; they feel tired and just want time for a break. This is Satan's plan; he wants us to turn our back on God's help. He wants us to feel secure so that he can control the battle and win. The question you need to ask yourself is why would you turn away when God has sent you to help to win?

Say to those who are fearful-hearts, "be strong, do not fear; your God will come, he will come with vengeance;   with divine retribution he will come to save you."

(Isaiah 35:4) NIV

ONE TRIP SHIP

The one trip ship is not a boat or ship. It is that first car you buy, the one that runs on hot days and rests on other days. The cost of the car could be money thrown out of the window. We may think about it as lasting until we can get something better, but do nothing to make it better. If we look at the big picture or into the future instead of what is in front of us now, we may see that by doing repairs and taking care of the vehicle, we may have it for years to come. Our teenagers can act this way. They can have the viewpoint that there is plenty of time to become a Christian. What is life if they do not sin or have a little fun? They think that it is no big deal and that they have a long time before they grow old. What is life without taking a few chances? We have an obligation to our children to set a good example for them to follow. As Christians, we know that it will be hard for us because of all the junk they learn in school or on the streets. That is why we must act, talk and instill that we are Christians. Our family life must revolve around God and His Word. Today we see divorce as an option, extra-marital affairs as common, unnatural relationships, and open sex as a game. If we are what we say, then we must act that way. The Bible does give us reason for divorce and that is adultery. There is warning about extra-marital affairs, un-natural sex, and pleasing of the flesh. God wiped out cities for less. If we do not understand what Our Lord wants and forget what we want, how can we expect our children to act like Christians? Be that example that God wants you to be!

Don't let anyone look down on you because you are young, but set an example for the believers in speech, in life, in love, in faith and in purity.

(1 Timothy 4:12) NIV

OPTION PACKAGE

Today's new cars and trucks come equipped two ways: a standard or the optional package. The standard package comes with just the basics. With the option package, you can get power windows, leather seats, cruise control, power seats, different types of radios and many other options. Each option will cost you above the standard package price of the vehicle. These options could cost you thousands of extra dollars, but with that extra cost, you receive more comforts. God also offers the standard plan for every person on earth. The standard plan comes with the gifts God gives everyone air, water, sun, moon, food and other items needed to survive. Option plan number 1 gives us salvation, peace, love, hope and happiness along with the knowledge that we will have everlasting life with the Lord. Option plan 2 gives everyone the opportunity to find salvation with the Lord; this plan is for the people that have not decided on option plan 1. The cost of option plan 1 is faith in the Lord Jesus Christ and accepting Him as our savior. We are also required to follow the life of a Christian as it is written in the Bible. The cost of failing to accepting option plan 1 is very simple; you will not have salvation with God! You will have a home or workplace with Satan in Hell. We all have a choice of what option plan to choose, it's all up to us on what we want to end up paying.

Should God then reward you on your terms, when you refuse to repent? You must decide, not I; so tell me what you know.
(Job 34:33) NIV

Over The Hill

How many times have you heard that once you reach a certain age you are considered over the hill? They say you are on the down side of life. Well, let God assure you that once you accept Jesus Christ as your savior in your life you are no longer on the down side of anything. When we accepted Jesus Christ as our savior, we have stepped over the mountain of the original sin that we came into this life with. We no longer need to feel sorry for getting old or being scared of dying, because what awaits us is the glory of heaven where age has no bearing. We can read in the Bible all the great wonders the Lord has waiting for us when we leave this life, as we know it. This is why we must share the word of God to our friends and neighbors so they also can find and accept Jesus Christ into their life. So the next time you have someone tell you that you are over the hill, tell him or her you crossed over the mountain not just the hill. Look at the surprised expression on their face, and if they ask why you said that, tell them.

Praise be to God and Father of our Lord Jesus Christ! In his great mercy he has given us new birth into a living hope through the resurrection of Jesus Christ from the dead.

(1 Peter 1:3) NIV

Payday

Most of us cannot wait for payday. After paying creditors and all the expenses we have, the money we have left over we can go buy a hot dog. We go throughout life working day to day to buy things we need to survive on and want. If we have a family, we try to provide the best we can for them. There are employers that have people working for them that enjoy their work and don't feel stressed about coming to work. There are other employers that the people who work for them dread showing up for work. However, both jobs pay us to work. There may be a difference in the amount of money we receive each payday, but we do get paid. We may look at changing to a different employer throughout our working careers for many reasons; it could be the pay or working conditions etc. Sometimes we may forget about the best employer we have, He gives us the best working conditions available to man and the greatest payday anyone could ask for. God is that employer! By following the word of God, our payday is right around the corner. We can go throughout our day with this knowledge and all the wonderful gifts He has given us. There is one other employer available to man and his name is Satan. He can give you great things here on earth; he can give you all the material gifts and wants of the flesh. You will think you have it made, but instead of receiving a payday when you are no longer of the flesh (dead), you will give Satan his payday. You will reside in Satan's workroom called Hell! Christians have a payday each and everyday here on earth and a bonus payday when we are no longer of this flesh! Do not forget to thank God for being the best employer you could ever ask for.

> The Lord is my light and my salvation – whom shall I fear? The Lord is my stronghold of my life – of whom shall I be afraid?
>
> (Psalm 27:1) NIV

PIECES OF STAINED GLASS

Beer, liquor and wine bottles are made with a form of stained glass. Many people find self-fulfilling happiness in these bottles. Some people use the ingredients in these bottles to escape from their life and problems. They believe that this is a solution, but the only solution to any problem is to face it instead of running or hiding from it. Our God can show everyone comfort, the problem may not go away but He will comfort us in dealing with them. There is other stain glass that also can be used to find happiness, which are the windows in the Lord's house. The stained glass windows in God's house allow His light to shine through, giving us a wonderful vision. Take a good look the next time you are in church, you will notice that there are hundreds of pieces of different colored glass making up the windows. The Christian family is also like that window; we come in different colors, sizes and shapes. When we come together, we also are a wonderful sight to each other and our Lord. The next time you see any stained glass, think about the wonderful stained glass in your church.

Keep watch over yourselves and all the flock of which the Holy Spirit has made you overseers. Be shepherds of the Church of God, which he bought with his own blood.

(Acts 20:28) NIV

PLAY ON WORDS

We sometimes use words that people take the wrong way. We call this playing on words. For example: you tell someone that his or her friend drinks a lot. They may think you are saying their friend drinks a lot of alcohol or beer. You just meant drinking water, coffee etc. This is a play on words. There are some words that you should never try to change their meaning; those are the Words of God. Below is a sample of His great Words.

The Ten Commandments

1 And God spoke all these words:
2 "I am the LORD your God, who brought you out of
Egypt, out of the land of slavery.
3 "You shall have no other gods before me.
4 "You shall not make for yourself an idol in the form of
anything in heaven above or on the earth beneath or in the
waters below. 5 You shall not bow down to them or worship
them; for I, the LORD your God, am a jealous God, punish-
ing the children for the sin of the fathers to the third and
fourth generation of those who hate me, 6 but showing love
to a thousand {generations} of those who love me and keep
my commandments.
7 "You shall not misuse the name of the LORD your God,
for the LORD will not hold anyone guiltless who misuses his
name.
8 "Remember the Sabbath day by keeping it holy. 9 Six days
you shall labor and do all your work, 10 but the seventh day

is a Sabbath to the LORD your God. On it you shall not do any work, neither you, nor your son or daughter, nor your manservant or maidservant, nor your animals, nor the alien within your gates. 11 For in six days the LORD made the heavens and the earth, the sea, and all that is in them, but he rested on the seventh day. Therefore the LORD blessed the Sabbath day and made it holy.

12 "Honor your father and your mother, so that you may live long in the land the LORD your God is giving you.

13"You shall not murder.

14 "You shall not commit adultery.

15 "You shall not steal.

16 "You shall not give false testimony against your neighbor.

17 "You shall not covet your neighbor's house. You shall not covet your neighbor's wife, or his manservant or maidservant, his ox or donkey, or anything that belongs to your neighbor."

18 When the people saw the thunder and lightning and heard the trumpet and saw the mountain in smoke, they trembled with fear. They stayed at a distance 19 and said to Moses, "Speak to us yourself and we will listen. But do not have God speak to us or we will die."

20 Moses said to the people, "Do not be afraid. God has come to test you, so that the fear of God will be with you to keep you from sinning."

21 The people remained at a distance, while Moses approached the thick darkness where God was.

(Exodus 20:1 – 20:21) NIV

Please Don't Give Up On Me

I know it seems as if I do not know what I want right now. Please do not give up on me, I love you and I am confused at this time. I know all the great things you do for me. I know that you love me and that you are trying to understand my actions. I am just so confused in what I want right now. I just need time to find myself. I do not know what direction to go. Lord, please show me the way back. I pray that you will not allow me to fail you. I beg you to clear the confusion from my mind and lead me to your goals. I am your child and ask you to take me under your wing and protect me from the evil one and all his followers. Please send all your angels to protect me. If I have failed you in some way, please forgive me for my sins. Lord I pray that you lead me out of temptation and back to the truth of your word.

I will search for the lost and bring back the strays. I will bind up the injured and strengthen the weak, but the sleek and the strong I will destroy. I will shepherd the flock with justice.

(Ezekiel 34:16) NIV

PLEASE, WHY?

You cannot have that. Get out of here. Go away. You have had enough. Don't do that. I do not care what you want. You are a loser. You do not need that. No. Many times the words we speak can hurt the people we say them to. When we use foul or inappropriate language and gestures, not only does this hurt others but both of these show how little we really are. Parents do have to be firm with their children at times, but we also give them the reason why and we should never act inappropriately. Using words of hate or inappropriate language is not only of the evil spirit but that of a sinner. There is no excuse ever to act this way as a Christian. Inappropriate behavior is not how God intended for us to act. Many people say they do it because they are mad or it's just a habit. The only reason that people act this way is that they do not have the Holy Spirit within them. True Christians may slip at times but not on a regular basis. If we should see a Christian act this way, it is our responsibility to let them know that inappropriate behavior is not acceptable in the eyes of the Lord.

The wicked desire the plunder of evil men, but the root of the righteous flourishes.

(Proverbs 12:12) NIV

Pleasing You

What a beautiful gesture. Don't you feel great when someone does something just to please you? When we go out of our way to do things for our loved ones and family, it's because we want to show them how much we care about them. The Bible is very clear on how we should live our lives as Christians. God shall be first in our life, then family and then all the rest. We start having problems when we forget this. We should not put anything in front of our Lord God. Sometimes we forget this and put our goals or wants ahead of what God wants for us. This causes us to rely on our own judgment and feeling that sometime leads us further away from God's wishes. When this happens, Satan is allowed to infiltrate our thoughts and this allows him to direct us with his wishes and not that of God's. We may not be aware that this is happening because of Satan's control over us. This is when our fellow Christians can help; they will see the change in our attitude and actions. We can be told a hundred times by twenty different fellow Christians that we are acting irrational, but until we see it in ourselves, we will dismiss their comments. When we are told this, we need to ask God for His direction, He will show us the truth! We must never underestimate the power of Satan in our life; this is why we must always put God first.

> Every word of God is flawless; he is a shield to those who take refuge in him. Do not add to his words, or he will rebuke you and prove you a liar.
>
> (Proverbs 30:5-6) NIV

Pure Truth at This Location

The Holy Bible should have a sign attached to it stating all information included is pure truth. With the Bible being written with God's direction and guidance how can anyone question the words that are written? We may question many things in our life, like what causes the sun to rise in the east and set in the west or why do we grow hair on our arms? We can find the answers too many of our questions by science, but do not be fooled in believing the creation of the world or anything in it is just an occurrence that just happened. Everything is a creation of God. The Bible is very clear to the creation of earth and everything on it. With all this information there still are people that question the power of God, some Christians also think they can interpret the words of the Bible to meet their wants. They tell themselves God does not know how the world operates now. Wrong, God knows everything as stated in the Bible. If we should have a question about anything, ask God for the answer, He will give us the truth to our question.

Guide me in your truth and teach me, for you are God my Savior, and my hope is in you all day long.

(Psalm 25:5) NIV

Put Me In, I'm Ready

Put me in, I am ready, I know what to do, I been waiting for this, I will make it, I am ready for anything. We go out into life with this type of attitude. There is nothing wrong with a positive attitude and outlook as long as we have God directing us. We may go into life and everything goes our way; but in most cases, we fall at some point. One of the big problems we see in today's culture is a large divorce rate. We make a commitment to marriage and it's not what we think it should be, and we are unhappy. The first thing that comes to our minds is divorce. God does not want any one of us to even consider divorce unless there is an act of marital unfaithfulness (Matthew 5:31). God did not promise life would be easy or without problems. He did promise that we could count on Him to comfort and guide us with His direction. The second problem is we try to add to God's words to what we want them to say. Some Christians think it is all right to read into the word of God as to what best suits there needs and wants. This type of attitude is wrong in the eyes of God and fellow Christians. We must trust Gods promise to see us through our falls; He will pick us up when we fall! When God came into our life and granted us salvation, He demands us to act as Christians not only when we want to, but all the time. You should continue your life with God in your heart and soul and when you fall, He is right there to pick you up. Now you are ready!

Jesus replied. "If anyone loves me, he will obey my teaching. My Father will love him, and we will come to him and make our home with him."
(John 14:23) NIV

QUIT LYING

Quit lying to me! This cannot be true! I do not deserve this! What did I do to have this happen to me? This doesn't happen to people like me! You are making a mistake! You may think that these words are coming from a person that just had something bad or wrong done to them. Wrong! These words can come from someone that feels they do not deserve the good things in life. When we are growing up, there can be issues or situations that cause us to feel we do not deserve anything that would let us be happy. Wrong again! God wants us to be happy in our life; He does not want us to feel that we do not deserve the good things in life. Being a Christian is the greatest happiness we can have, so if God gives us that, why can't we be happy with ourselves? Satan! There are two powers working here on earth. The first is God—He wants all His children to be happy. Then there is Satan, his goal is to disrupt and destroy all that God has given us. This could cause us some real unrest in our life, we know what we have is good; the question we keep asking ourselves is why are we unhappy? The answer could be as easy as us forgiving ourselves for the past because God has forgiven us. The other answer could be our lie-based memories; this is a lie that Satan stirs up in us causing us to be unhappy. This is when we need God's help in overcoming these lie-based memories. There are Christians that are trained in helping us, as long as we seek the truth and happiness that God wants us to have. God stands by us, so why don't we stand by Him? Remember He wants us to be happy, so let's give Him what He wants.

> Are not angels ministering spirits sent to serve those who will inherit salvation?
>
> (Hebrews 1:14) NIV

RESULTS

We do everything wanting results. We work and want to be paid. We workout at the gym we want to be healthy. We, we, we, it's always about what we want. We do this and we want this. We expect to have results for what we do now. Thank God, He is not this way. He gave us His only Son, Jesus Christ, so "we" can have salvation! When things go wrong in our life, we want God to fix it right now! Don't hold your breath! God will do what is right in His own time and not on our time schedule. If we want it our way, go to a fast food restaurant and order something. We cannot put conditions on God's help. Christians must remember God is with us for the long run. God made a commitment to us and He will stand by that. We, as Christians, also make commitments and we also must stand by them. Before we ask why we did not get the results that we wanted, we need to look at what we did to not warrant them. If we only put in half the effort and expect 100% results, we are being self-deceiving. If we want God's help in a problem, give the problem to Him. He will give us results on His time schedule, not ours. We must not try to act in haste, because the results may not be what we or God wants. Remember to take "we" out of the picture and put in what God wants instead.

Therefore, my people will know my name; therefore in that day they will know that it is I who foretold it. Yes, it is I.

(Isaiah 52:6) NIV

Self Service

In today's culture, we see less of the customer service and more of the self-service style establishments. There are self-service gas stations, grocery stores, convince stores, retail stores and even eating establishments. We do most, if not all, of the work and then pay for the opportunity. The reason they can have self-service is because we allow it. Some establishments have strong "we serve the customer" attitude such as hospitals, banks, and jewelry stores. We know why hospitals have this attitude; can you see someone operating on him or herself? Bank and jewelry stores just do not trust us. God has established being a Christian as a self-service and a full service program. God will not force us to accept Jesus Christ as our savior, He does not threaten us, we must do this on our own accord. We decide to accept Jesus as our savior and then we must follow the word of God and practice being a Christian. God then gives us the full service of His grace, love, understanding and, most of all, forgiveness for our sins so that we have everlasting life with Him. The self-service part is how we fellowship, go to church, and share the word of God with others. This is only a small fraction of His full and self-service programs that help us throughout our life as a Christian.

Therefore, as we have opportunity, let us do good to all people, especially to those who belong to the family of believers.

(Galatians 6:10) NIV

Shining Through the Trees

Mother Nature is one of the greatest creations God has given us. We can go anywhere on this planet and by just opening our eyes, we can see God's wonders. Imagine walking a trail leading us to the top of a mountain. The trail could lead us though grasslands, rock formations and wooded areas. We can see all types of wildlife and plants on our journey. The deeper we enter the woods the darker it becomes, because of the trees blocking out some of the light. We can still see our way along the trail with the sunlight that penetrates through. Christians also travel the trail of salvation that God has set out for us. We could also come upon times in our life when some of the Lord's light becomes blocked. This is when we need to stop what we are doing and examine what is causing this. When we feel that our life is in the darkest of the night with no light, we must not forget that the Lord's light is always shining for us. We need to ask the Lord for directions so that we could feel His full light in our heart and soul again. Let us not forget that as long as the sun is in the sky, there will be light of the sun shining through the trees.

You are my lamp, O Lord; the Lord turns my darkness into light.

(2 Samuel 22:29) NIV

SNAKE IN THE HEN HOUSE

What a shame, you go to the hen house to get your daily supply of eggs. You check each nest and found no eggs. You tell yourself it's just one day without eggs, no big deal. The next four days are the same, no eggs. Now you start thinking what could be wrong: the feed, hens are too old or that the rooster is not performing. You review all the facts and common factors that could be the problem. You come to the conclusion that the rooster is the problem, it is just not performing. The next morning you go to your neighbor's ranch and buy a strong young roster. That night you have the old rooster for dinner. Christians can act like the rancher, knowing that they have problems in their life and look for all the possible causes. They come up with what must be the problem, so they take actions to eliminate the problem as they see fit. A few weeks go by and every thing seems fine. Then one day the snake comes back for your eggs. He left for a short time to eat the eggs from your neighbors hens. But guess what? "It's back." Christians need to trust God to handle their problem; He will guide us in the right direction. Christians should not act like the rancher. We should not look for conclusions on our own, without God's direction. Would it not be a shame to eliminate the wrong thing and still have the problem?

> Come back to your senses as you ought, and stop sinning; for there are some who are ignorant of God – I say this to your shame.
>
> (1 Corinthians 15:34) NIV

Sponging

God created us in His image. He did not give us the knowledge and information we need to know to survive all at once. God did give us the means of learning by giving us a brain. Our brain starts absorbing information the second we are conceived. Think of our brain as a sponge. It will absorb until it is filled. I do not think our brain will ever get to a point of not being able to absorb information. We go through life absorbing information— both to survive and to make choices. We absorb both the good and bad experiences. We decide that we are going to accept Jesus Christ as our savior and we become a Christian. We ask and receive forgiveness from God for our past sins. Sometimes we let our past memories reappear in the present. We sometimes have trouble remembering that God forgave us and wonder why we can't forgive ourselves. God does not want us to keep reliving our past pains. He wants us to live for Him and enjoy all of His gifts. This is where Satan comes into play. He will do everything in His power to disrupt our pleasure with the Lord. He will tell us lies about ourselves, such as we do not deserve what God has given us. He will use our past memories against us. We must remember that God has given us the gift of everlasting life and all the good things we have now. We must leave the past in the past and live for God enjoying all He has given us.

> And the LORD God made all kinds of trees grow out of the ground-trees that were pleasing to the eye and good for food. In the middle of the garden were the tree of life and the tree of the knowledge of good and evil.
>
> (Genesis 2:9) NIV

THE 18-INCH QUESTION

Do you feel that you are a Christian? Did you know that there are at least two types of Christians? One type of Christian is that with the knowledge of God's Word (book smart), but they do not apply the knowledge they have to their heart and soul. They miss the mark by 18 inches to the brain and to the heart and soul. We call this type of Christian a Pretend- Christian. How can you tell this? Easy. This type of Pretend-Christian will read and preach the Word. They will add or read only what suits their needs in God's Word. They will avoid other Christians that can see through their lies. They will avoid fellowshipping with the family of God. They will seem sincere with their belief, only to the extent of personal gain. This type of Pretend-Christian will not lead by example, but only by words. They will not have joy in their life, because they do not have the true seed of God in their heart and soul. They will miss heaven's gate by 18 inches. The other type of Christian is easy to recognize. They will be filled with happiness in knowing that they have God's word within their heart and soul. They will still have conflicts within their life, but they have the knowledge that God will prevail. They listen and act according to God's directions without question. They look forward to fellowshipping with other Christians. They love to talk the Word of God to family and friends. They do not avoid church. They look forward to going and they lead by example, not by mere words. We call this type of Christian a True-Christian. The everlasting life question is "What type of Christian are you?"

The one who received the seed that fell among the thorns is the man who hears the word, but the worries of this life and the deceitfulness of wealth choke it, making it unfruitful. But the one who received the seed that fell on good soil is the man who hears the word and understands it. He produces a crop, yielding a hundred, sixty or thirty times what was sown."

(Matthew 13:22 & 13:23) NIV

THE BIG GAME

There's plenty of time left, just keep telling yourself that to keep going and everything will work out. Five, four, three, two, one— the game is over. You think to yourself that it was a real quick game. It flew by. Let's review the game tape; we take a long look at the game and notice that on many occasions, we didn't do much to help ourselves out. We also notice that it seemed like we were helping the opponents to some degree. We brush this game off and tell ourselves we'll do better next game. Wrong! The game you were just in was the game of life. You are dead and the tapes you reviewed were how you acted in life. There are no second games or chances. It's over. Now it's time to pay the price. Everyday that we take a breath of air is a day that we will have to answer for. We can feel that we have time to change or correct wrongs that we have committed, but who is keeping the time clock on our life? Our life can be altered forever in one second. We could lose a loved one or someone close to us at any second. Any second we could be gone forever too. That is why God has given us His word to live by, so that we don't regret losing out on life. We have that guarantee of everlasting life with Him. If we think we need to make changes, we had better start right this second because we don't know how many more seconds we have left. God has given us the gift of life and at any time, he can take it away.

Keep his decrees and commands, which I am giving you today, so that
it may go well with you and your children after you and that you may
live long in the land the LORD your God gives you for all time.

(Deuteronomy 4:40) NIV

The Buffet

We can go to most restaurants these days and they will have some sort of buffet. These buffets are full of many choices of foods, desserts, and drinks. There are healthy and some not so healthy foods to choose from. In addition, there is no limit on how much we can consume. The best part is we only pay one set price for all of this. Most of us go with the intention that we will consume at least, if not more, than the cost of the meal. We want as much as possible for our money. Our life is like a buffet, we have so many things to choose from— like where we live, what type of job we have, what level of education we want, along with thousands of other choices. There will be some choices that we would like to make but because of reasons beyond our control, we are unable to. There are many of us that choose the path of the Lord and all the gifts He offers us with His buffet. The gift of the Fruit of the Spirit is for us to feed on and there is no limit to what we can consume. When we walk with the Fruit of the Spirit within us God is there to guide us. When we act without the Fruit of the Spirit, Satan's influence and distractions, can and will, attack us at every turn. Christians must always eat from Gods buffet and avoid the temptations from Satan's kitchen.

But the fruit of the Spirit is love, joy, peace, patience, kindness, goodness, faithfulness, gentleness and self-control. Against such things there is no law.

(Galatians 5:22) NIV

THE CROSS ROADS

Throughout life, we will come upon many crossroads in our path that we will need to decide if we should go straight, turn left or turn right. Sometimes we do not have a choice in this because of circumstances outside of our control. In this type of situation, we need to make the best we can of it. Christians are not exempt of having to choose which direction to travel, because God may have a plan for our future that is unknown to us. When we come upon a crossroad and do not know what to do, this is the time we need to pray for God's direction. We must insure that this is God's plan and not that of Satan's. Remember that Satan can come appearing as God to lead us astray. This is where faith and believing in God's word as it is written in the Bible will guide us in the right direction. Do not be fooled by Satan's words, for he is not that of good and righteousness. We may feel at the time our choice in correct and find out later that Satan has deceived us. God does not what any of us to fall into Satan's trap, which is why we have fellow Christians to inform us that we are being deceived. We may not accept the fact that they say this to us, because we do not see ourselves as they see us. This will cause us to be confused and upset with the people trying to help us. God works in strange ways and one of those ways is for other Christians to intervene. Trust in the Lord our God for He will lead us out of temptation.

"Watch and pray so that you will not fall into temptation. The spirit is willing, but the body is weak."

(Matthew 26:41) NIV

THE DOORS

You are walking down the street and notice up ahead what seems like a line of people. The closer you get, you see people forming three lines. You decide that you don't have time for this and try to cross to the other side of the street, but you can't because of a tall fence you didn't see a second ago.

Now you have no choice but to continue. The closer you get you notice that one line is longer than the other two; looking around you discover why. There above each line is a sign. The first sign says "Christians," the second sign says " Non-Christians," and the third sign says "Undecided." Now you know why the one line is so long. It is the Christian line. You know that's your line! You reach the front of line to find a person sitting at a table. You think to yourself – "there is no way that this person is a Christian. This person has tattoos, earrings, ratty clothes and he smells." The person behind the table asks you to empty everything from your pockets. They look at everything. They see the pictures of your family, the notes to buy diapers, the doctor appointment slips, cash, etc. Then the person picks up a bag of what looks like dried grass, a pipe, some needles and some little rocks. He looks at you and smiles. At the next table, the person behind it hands you a pen and a questionnaire; you start to fill it out but the pen doesn't seem to write all the time, so you do the best you can, leaving some areas blank. Looking around you see three doors: one black, one wood and one of gold. You notice that there are quite a few people going in the wood and gold doors; you think to yourself the gold door must be heaven and the wood door hell. The person at the end of the line directed you to the gold door; you feel great. You open the door and you are astonished at what you see, smell and at the sounds you hear. You are just overwhelmed. Wake up; wake up are you all right? You awakened with the smell of sulfur in your nose, the feeling of fire in your eyes and the sounds of screaming in your ears. Christians do not know when that day is coming. If we think we are doing what God wants us to do, great! If you're not sure or have any questions on your behavior or actions, now is the time to change. For the rules and regulations of salvation, all you need to do is read the rulebook; that's the Bible. The directions on the form stated it had to be completely filled out to be accepted into heaven. We also need to follow all of God's Words and directions, not just what we want to follow.

> Act according to the law they teach you and the decisions they give you. Do not turn aside from what they tell you, to the right or to the left.
>
> (Deuteronomy 17:11) NIV

THE DRIVER

We love the freedom to hop in our vehicle and go places when we want. Sometimes this is not so much a freedom but a requirement. When we have small children, as parents we have the honor to take them to after school practices, dances, shopping, along with many other places. We do this out of love, as we want our children to have fun and do things with their friends. The time will come when they grow up and no longer need their parents to be the driver. They will be on their own and have the freedom to hop in their own vehicle and go places when they want. We may feel left out, but this is part of our children's growing up process. God does not intend on parents to control their children's lives. We, as parents, need to plant the seed of God in them and then pray that they seek the gifts of God and let Him grow within their heart and soul. We can support this process by being great examples of Christians to our children. We must remember actions speak louder than words. God is the driver of our life and our children's lives. He wants us to be like a road sign, showing the way to God for them.

Children's children are a crown to the aged, and parents are the pride of their children.

(Proverbs 17:6) NIV

The Fact of the Matter

As a Christian, what did we do today to deserve the gifts the Lord has given us? Did we go out of our way to tell someone thanks for there help? Did we call someone just to tell them we miss them and are praying for them? Did we say good morning or afternoon to a stranger? Did we do something special for our family? Did we thank God for everything He has given us? Did we tell someone that we love them? Did we read out of the Bible today? Did we share the word of God with someone? Did we act in accordance with God's law? We can go throughout the day acting as if we are on an island and nothing matters except what we want. We can ask ourselves "why be nice to a stranger, what can they do to help us?" We sometimes forget that all we have is because God gave it all to us. Christians need to never forget that we are ambassadors of God. Our actions are a direct reflection of God's words.

A wicked messenger falls into trouble, but a trustworthy envoy brings health.

(Proverbs 13:17) NIV

THE GETAWAY

An out-of-the way riverbank can be a very relaxing location if we just want to sit, watch and listen to the water pass by. The banks lined with trees, showing their fall colors, can be beautiful and soothing to the heart and soul. God gave us all of this beauty for us to enjoy. We can also learn from just watching the water pass by. Think about every second of time that passes by in our life. We are unable to turn back one second. The water flowing by us is like our life. Once it passes by, there is nothing that can be done to return it to its start. It is imperative that we make each and every second count in our life. We may be unable to correct the wrongs we committed in the past, but we can insure that we do not repeat our mistakes. God will forgive us for all of our past sins. Think about the trees lining the banks. Their roots are well secured within the ground. Christians also should have their belief in God well rooted like the trees along the banks. Like the trees, Christians can show their beautiful colors throughout life.

"Like valleys they spread out, like gardens beside a river, like aloes planted by the LORD, like cedars beside the waters.
(Numbers 24:6) NIV

The Pair Of …

We can read in the Bible that God created man and all the creatures on earth. Adam had the honor to name all of them. Each one had a mate but Adam. God created women from Adam and now all creatures had a mate. This was God's wish for man to have a woman as his mate. Marriage is Gods gift to man and woman, to come together as one to multiply the earth. When a man and women join in marriage, it is God's doings. God states what He has joined together no man shall undo. The Bible is very precise on what grounds a man and woman can divorce. Today's culture has made it so easy for the separation of man and women that it is not only a failure to the marriage, but also a disgrace to God. If we need to separate something, try socks, shoes, glasses or anything else that comes in pairs. But do not separate what God has joined. Surrender yourself to the Lord and trust him one hundred percent for direction and comfort.

Marriage should be honored by all, and the marriage bed kept pure, for God will judge the adulterer and all the sexually immoral. Keep your lives free from the love of money and be content with what you have, because God has said "Never will I leave you; never will I forsake you."

(Hebrews 13:4 - 13:5) NIV

The Path

Why do you let the evil one direct you to the path of thorns and thickets? Do you not feel the thorns pierce your heart, and the thickets scratching your skin? Have I not taken you from the path of the evil one? Have I not answered your prayers of life when you asked? Why then do you let the evil one darken your heart with his thoughts? Have I not blessed you and your love ones with My Word? Why then do you seek the path with the evil one? Why have you not seen My light? Have I not sent you My messengers? Why do you ignore what I have given you? Awake My child and come to Me. Do not let the evil one deceive you any more! I have shown you the path to glory and everlasting life. I have given you the blessings you desire. Why do you not hear Me? Awake and return to the path of rightness. The path of the evil one will leave you like an island in the ocean all alone. My child, return to your family for that is My wish! Awake from the darkness of the evil one! Seek and find My light for I miss you.

"Do not let your hearts be troubled. Trust in God; trust also in me."

(John 14:1) NIV

THE POOL

You look out the kitchen window and you see your family pool; it's not what you really wanted. Your dream pool is twice the size and has a diving board and a slide. You also notice your yard is not what you really want either. You think to yourself that there are many things you really don't like. You look over at your neighbor's house and notice that they have a great pool, nice yard and many of the things you want. A few days later, your neighbor asks you if you would keep an eye on their house because they are going out of town for a few days. You tell them no problem. You can't get the thoughts out of your mind that you really are not happy with what you have. You decide what you want and you're going to have it even if it's for a short time. You change into your swimsuit and go to the neighbor's back yard. You feel the soft grass under you feet and think it's great. You decide that you're going to try out their pool, so you climb the ladder to the diving board and run off the board to do a triple flip. As you are twisting in the air, you notice something very strange. NO WATER IN THE POOL! You're committed; no turning back. Christians may think at times that their life is without meaning or direction. God always has a direction for us; His direction is for our salvation. Satan will attempt to distract us by putting thoughts in our minds telling us life is better over there. If we fail to see this and act like the person on the diving board, where do you think we will end up? Happy or sad, heaven or hell, family or alone it is your choice— make the right one.

"Watch and pray so that you will not fall into temptation. The spirit is willing, but the body is weak."

(Matthew 26:41) NIV

The Roof is Leaking

The roof is leaking. Get some buckets or pots to catch the water. This could be a problem, but only when it rains. What would we do if it doesn't rain for three months? We could put off the repairs until it rains again or should we call someone to repair the roof before it becomes worse. We can also act this way when we have problems in our daily living. We put off addressing the problem until it is a major issue. When we have a problem in our life, we need to address it and not just keep putting it off. We need to be responsible for our actions not only to others, but also to God. By putting issues off, we are being irresponsible. We sometimes don't ask God for help until issues or problems are too large for us to deal with. If we ask God for daily directions, this may eliminate small issues becoming large issues. This is why it is so important for us to not only say we are Christians, but also practice what we preach. The next time something needs repair…get to it.

The king replied, "If the LORD does not help you, where can I get help for you? From the threshing floor? From the winepress?"

(2 Kings 6:27) NIV

THE SKY IS FALLING

We as Christians will have times in our lives when it feels as if the sky is falling on our head and there are no shelters for us to seek safety. We must not forget that this is the time that we need Jesus Christ in our life. We need to seek the safety of His open arms, for He will shield us from danger. We may not know why these things are happening to us, but we must trust in the Lord. We must not put the blame for this on the Lord or any others. We are only of the flesh and being so, we can be misled by the evil one to do or act in ways the Lord does not want us to. We must not keep questioning why these things are happening or what we did wrong to deserve this. We must pray to the Lord and ask Him for comfort in our time of need. As it is written in Proverbs 15:29, "The Lord is far from the wicked but He hears the prayer of the righteous". Pray to the Lord and He will see you through this time of need. He will comfort you when you need comforting.

"I have told you these things, so that in me you may have peace. In this world you will have trouble. But take heart! I have overcome the world."

(John 16:33) NIV

THE SLIPPERY STEP

"Caution slip hazard," "Slippery when wet" and "icy conditions use caution" are all warning signs we may see around us. When floors or steps are wet, there is a chance they will become slippery. When it's cold out, rain can turn sidewalks and roadways icy or the rain can turn to snow. This can cause driving or walking to be very dangerous. We depend on others to place warning signs or to salt and clean sidewalks and roadways. Christians depend on Jesus Christ for our salvation. If it was not for Him being crucified, we could not have salvation with our Lord. When we have problems in our life, we sometime seek help from the wrong source, we may believe that this source is reliable and sincere in their recommendations or suggestions. If we seek help from any other source than God, we are headed down a slippery step. God gives us fellow Christians that are trained in dealing with our problems; they will counsel us within the guidelines of God's words and wishes. If we should follow the advice that leads us away from the Word of God, how can we say that we are Christians? Pray to our God that we follow His word without question, because this is the wish of our Lord.

Not everyone who says to me, "Lord, Lord", will enter the kingdom of Heaven, but only he who does the will of my Father who is in heaven.

(Matthew 7:21) NIV

THE STONE OR ROCK

We see the use of stones and rocks every day. They are used in decorating yards, walkways and buildings. Many types of rings and jewelry have stone inserts. Jewels are used as adornment for rings and necklaces because of their value and beauty. Man used rocks and stones for building homes and forts for safety and protection. Rocks or large stones were used as markers for property lines. Rocks and stones are very easily found in most areas. Farmers plowing their fields move them to a stone or rock pile. This is because they can damage their equipment or restrict crops from growing. There is one stone that we see used at most cemeteries. This is the headstone on a gravesite. This stone is intended to last for many years to inform others of who is buried. This marker also may have a few words telling a short story about that person. These words can be the last words written about that person. Would it not be great if every one of these head stones read that this person was a Christian and is now in the comfort of heaven with our Father? We can write or say anything about the deceased but if their name is not written in God's book, they will not see the glory of heaven. When we are dead, the clock stops and no matter what is said or written about us will change were we will go. We need to make that decision now while we are living. Do you know where you are headed?

"He who has an ear, let him hear what the Spirit says to the churches. He who overcomes shall not be hurt by the second death"

(Revelation 2:11) NIV

THE UNKNOWN SHOPPER

Would you love to go shopping and find everything you want at one location and when you were finished shopping, you found no long lines to wait in? Sure you would! Now add in the fifty percent discount you receive. Now you are having a great shopping trip. The clerk informs you that from this point on you will receive ninety percent or more every time you shop at their store. They also tell you that if they do not have what you want, they will get it for you at no cost. You feel this is too good to be true, so you ask what the catch is. They tell you that you need to talk to the storeowner, but he not available at this time, but he did put it in writing. You read the letter and all that is required is that you only shop at his store. You agree that you will do that. You think to yourself what a great deal you have. Now the greatest of news, God offers us one hundred percent salvation for accepting Jesus Christ as our savor. That unknown shopper is known as a Christian.

Because of this oath, Jesus has become the guarantee of a better covenant.

(Hebrews 7:22) NIV

THE WALKING BILLBOARD

Christians go through life as carpenters, lawyers, doctors, roofers, nurses, and every other profession on earth. Each one of these Christians is a walking billboard for Christ. They are the neon message in the night of what the love of God has done for them. God wants us to share His word with others, but most of all He wants us to walk and talk as true Christians. Like any message, if we falter in our actions not only do we miss the mark, we are showing the wrong message of how a Christian should conduct themselves. We are to be an example to our family, friends and everyone else. There will be those posing as Christians, but in reality they are nothing more then actors. These actors will say that they are Christians with their words, but their heart and soul is not filled with the Holy Spirit of God. Thus, their actions are not what God wants advertised as His words. The big question is, are you a billboard for God or a billboard for the evil one? You cannot be both!

The LORD said to me: "What they say is good. I will raise up for them a prophet like you from among their brothers; I will put my words in his mouth, and he will tell them everything I command him. If anyone does not listen to my words that the prophet speaks in my name, I myself will call him to account. But a prophet who presumes to speak in my name anything I have not commanded him to say, or a prophet who speaks in the name of other gods, must be put to death."

(Deuteronomy 18:17 - 18:20) NIV

This for That

I will do that for you if you do this for me. The great barter system at work. This system is based on you doing one thing for someone, then in return they do something for you. The rules are simple. An example of this may be that you mow a neighbor's yard and you agree that it would cost ten dollars. That neighbor would then owe you some form of service that equals ten dollars. This system requires no exchanging of money, just services. Some people join a club that deals with a barter system; they keep records and ledgers on who owes whom. Christians also belong to a type of barter system where God gives us everlasting life and all His gifts and all we have to do is have faith in Him and His words as written in the Holy Bible. If you look at this deal, we come out winners, because there is no way we can equal what God offers us. Christians should go through life helping our fellow neighbors without looking or expecting some form of pay back. We must beware of people using us in the wrong way because we are Christians. Sometime Satan will use us to further his cause by letting us feel we are helping others when in fact he is leading us away from God. If we feel at any time that our actions are that of the evil one, we should check our actions to see if we are living God's word.

And we know that in all things God works for the good of those who love him, to who have been called according to his purpose.
(Romans 8:28) NIV

This Side Up

We see this on boxes, packages and other items— the reason they mark items this way is because it could be turned upside down and cause damage to the product. There are many things we should use common sense about and not turn upside down. A pie or an opened can of soda are examples. How about a Christmas tree? This is one of the items we display during Christmas. Have you ever seen a Christmas tree placed upside down? The Christmas tree is a beautiful symbol of Christmas. Many homes have them to celebrate this wonderful day in the life of Christians. This is the birth of Jesus Christ our savior . We can place an angel or star on top of our tree, and add all types of ornaments to enhance its beauty. Take a good look at the tree and you will see that it is pointing to Heaven. Christians should always look to the heavens and our Lord, not only during the Christmas season, but also during every day of our life. Throughout the year we can see God's plants shooting from the ground pointing to the heavens. So raise your hands, heart and soul to the heavens, and thank God for His gift of salvation.

The angel of the Lord encamps around those who fear him, and he delivers them. Taste and see that the Lord is good; blessed is the man who takes refuge in him.

(Psalm 34:7 & 34:8) NIV

TITLE

We will go through life with some type of title. It could be a job title, like roofer, cook, banker, actor or police officer. Some titles do not require a person to think about what it means. Take the title of the President of the United States. Most people around the world would know who this is. They may not know his name, but they will know what he represents. When we accept Jesus into our life, we also take on a title. Our title is that of "Christian." With this title, we take on a completely new job description. Our title and job description are for life while here on earth. We also have accepted new responsibility, not only for ourselves, but that of our fellow Christians, family, and friends. When someone asks you if you are a Christian and you say yes, there is no question what you represent. Christians represent God and all of His greatness in the world. You represent that believing in Him and following His word will bring everlasting salvation. Therefore, the next time a title sounds impressive, remember the title of Christian is given to you by the grace of God.

We have heard with our ears, O God; our fathers have told us
what you did in their days, in days long ago.

(Psalm 44:1) NIV

Tour Available
Without Reservation

All types of business and resorts offer tours of their locations. Some require that we make reservations in advance and some just let us show up. When we go on these tours, we get the grand treatment. They may provide transportation, meals and some spending money. The purpose of the tours is to inform us of what's available for a cost. Their goal is to have us feel their products or services are well worth the money they are charging. Would non-believers love to be able to tour heaven to see all the wonderful gifts offered? There would be no non-believers around after the tour of heaven. They could see what they are getting before they have to do anything. Christians do not require a tour because they know the truth of God's word and they accepted Jesus Christ as their savior, they know what is waiting for them in heaven. I think a better tour for non-believer would be a tour of hell, after that let them decide what they want. By the way, Heaven does require an advanced reservation. To receive your advanced reservation all you need to do is accept Jesus Christ as your savior.

> Yours, O LORD, is the greatness and the power and the glory and the majesty and the splendor, for everything in heaven and earth is yours. Yours, O LORD, is the kingdom; you are exalted as head over all.
>
> (1 Chronicles 29:11) NIV

Toxic Mess

Warning! We have a toxic situation present! This form of toxic mess is not detectable by any form of technical equipment. Spreading is not limited to any age, race, sex or location. It is widespread over all the earth at this time. Failure to pay attention to this warning could cause injury or death. All precautions must be taken to limit contact. There is a vaccine available for total recovery if a person has been infected. There is also a preventive measure that will eliminate contracting any form of this toxic mess. The vaccine and preventive measures can be taken at any time. It is recommended that the sooner it be taken, the better the survival rate. The vaccine is the Word of God and accepting Jesus Christ as your Savior. Believing in God and everything He stands for will give us total immunity from Satan. The toxic mess is that of Satan's influence on us if we allow it. We will sin in our lifetime, but believing in God's Holy Word and asking for forgiveness will allow us everlasting life with Him. Vaccines are located in the Bible and the house of God. If you need directions to these locations, please contact the nearest Christian. If this is an emergency, please contact God directly. God's vaccine is available all the time throughout your life.

Worship the LORD your God, and his blessing will be on your food and water. I will take away sickness from among you.

(Exodus 23:25) NIV

VISITS

We, as Christians, will visit many places and people in our lifetime. Whom we visit and where we go is what we need to look at. In today's culture, it is easy for people to get lost in all the glitter and lights. We go to the gas station for gas, the grocery store for food, or the shoe store for shoes. We go to the Lord's house for spiritual uplifting and fellowshipping. We have read in the Bible where Jesus visited many places. Whenever Jesus went somewhere, He always had a purpose. This was to teach and spread the word of God. When we go to visit, we also need to have a purpose for going. Sometimes we feel like staying at home and just relaxing, but Christians need to act like our Lord and share the Word of God on our visits. We do not need to read scripture or preach to spread His Word. We can share our Christian beliefs by our actions. So the next time you go for a visit, do not forget to share.

He humbled you, causing you to hunger and then feeding you with manna, which neither you nor your fathers had known, to teach you that man does not live on bread alone but on every word that comes from the mouth of the LORD.

(Deuteronomy 8:3) NIV

Wake Up Call

We go to bed and then we wake. Sometimes we need a wake up call or we may oversleep and miss an appointment or an important meeting. Christians may need a wake up call from God if they start to stray from His word. We may feel that we are not straying at all from Him and we do not need a wake up call. All Christians will stray from God in their lifetime. The degree to which we stray is the question. We may not even know we are straying, because we do it a little bit at a time. Before we know it, we have strayed more than we thought. This is the time we need a wake up call from God. How would a Christian know if they have strayed or are straying? They could know by their actions. Some examples would be using foul language, dressing inappropriately and visiting pornographic sites, bars, nightclubs or any other places that could cause them to sin. Maybe it is the friends or hours they keep, etc. They also may stop or reduce reading the Word of God. The people close to them can see the changes, but in most cases they do not know what to do or say. They may say it's none of their business. If they are a Christian, they have the obligation to their friend and to God to make mention of the changes they see – to give a wake up call.

> Be careful, however, that the exercise of your freedom does not become a stumbling block to the weak. For if anyone with a weak conscience sees you who have this knowledge eating in an idol's temple, won't he be emboldened to eat what has been sacrificed to idols?
>
> (1 Corinthians 8:9 & 8:10) NIV

WALKING ON WATER

We read in the Bible that Jesus walked on water. We can only walk on water when it is frozen. Unlike Jesus, we need to have the water frozen so that we do not sink. Before we proceed to walk on a frozen river, we check the thickness of the ice. We sometimes think the ice is thick enough to hold our weight. We sometimes fail to take into consideration that the undercurrents could cause it to appear to be solid and in reality, only the surface is frozen. If we proceed without caution, we may end up falling into the frigid waters. When we look at fellow Christians, they also my appear to be solid followers of Christ, but do not be deceived by their outer appearance. There are deceivers among us that speak the word of God, but in their heart they have unholy motives. Christians must be aware that not all professed Christians are that of God. We must look at their actions along with hearing the words they speak to know if this person is in fact a follower of God. Let us not be fooled by their false words and action that can lead us away from God. Beware!

"Watch out for false prophets, they come to you in sheep's clothing, but inwardly they are ferocious wolves."
(Matthew 7:15) NIV

Warning Whistle and Lights

My child, why do you not take notice of the train whistle and warning lights? Do you not hear the whistle warning you of the danger coming to you? Why do you not see the warning lights flashing in front of you? Do you not see the lights? Why do you continue your path of destruction and death? What must I do to save you from the danger of the train? Why have you not learned the dangers of the train that I taught you? Have I not shown you them correctly? My child, stop and come back to Me. My arms are open for you. Wake up and hear me calling you. Please, I beg you to come away from the train; you are no match for the power and destruction that it will cause you.

The prudent see danger and take refuge, but the simple keep it going and suffer for it.

(Proverbs 27:12) NIV

Weeds on the Wire

Have you ever noticed that weeds grow everywhere? They grow in all the spots you don't want them to, like up power poles and even on the guide wires that hold the pole straight. They can weave between the holes in fences, up flagpoles in our flowerbeds and lawns. We may think they are only weeds, but take a good look at them. They each have their own quality. Ivy is considered by some as a weed. However, many people let it grow all over their fences and up their walls and feel it adds character. They all have a few things in common. The first is that God creates them all. The second is they all started from a seed. If you notice, they all try to grow upward towards Heaven, and they are not easy to get rid of. They keep returning. Christians deal with a form of weed called sin. Sin has some of the same characteristics as weeds, such as it's all over the place. Some people think there is nothing wrong with sinning and it always comes back. Once it gets started, it is hard to get rid of. Christians do have an insecticide that will work at destroying their weeds. There is a danger using this insecticide (AJCAYS) because of its side affects. It will cause a person to be saved and have everlasting salvation with God. The main ingredients are "Accepting Jesus Christ As Your Savior" and following the Word of God.

Jesus told them another parable: "The kingdom of heaven is like a man who sowed good seed in his field."
(Matthew 13:24) NIV

Weekly Check Up

It is time to have our weekly check-up. Let us open our minds, heart, and soul to the Lord. This exam should not hurt, but if you do have any pain or discomfort, God has something for you. Let us start with a few questions and we will go from there.

Question One:
In the past seven days how many times have you read the word of God?

Question Two:
In the last week, did you inform God of what your plans are?

Question Three:
During the past week, did you thank God for everything He has given you?

Question Four:
Did you stray from God's direction, commit sinful acts, or have sinful thoughts?

Question Five:
How often did you fellowship with your family this week?

Question Six:
Are you proud of your actions of the past week?

Question Seven:
Do you feel closer to God's teaching this week compared
to last week?

Question Eight:
Did you ask God to forgive your sins that you committed?

Final Question:
As a child of God, would you want our Lord to judge
you on your actions of the past week?

This concludes the question part of this check up.

DIAGNOSIS:

Looking at the results, it is recommended that you sit back and take inventory of your life. We, as Christians, know what is right in the eyes of the Lord. We all sin, God knows that and He will forgive us. If you feel in your heart and soul that you are doing what God expects of you, continue that course of action.

PRESCRIPTION:

If you are feeling a little discomfort, please take a dose of God's Word as needed throughout the day. If you should have any questions, please contact God. He is available 24 hours, 7 days a week.

CAUTION:

Side effects of these include habit-forming happiness, love and salvation. Failure to follow this will include sadness, confusion, loneliness, and a possible feeling of sitting in a pool of hot sulfur.

What Does It Feel Like?

How do you think it feels to turn your back on God's Word and directions? Many Christians know how this feels although they may not realize it at the time. Satan is very clever and subtle in leading us away from God's Word. Satan knows that by doing this a little bit at a time, we may not notice the slight changes. We will at some point realize that Satan and his ways have deceived us. We could lose things that we hold close and dear to us. God does send us warnings that we are straying from Him, but most of the time we ignore them. Fellow Christians also try to inform us that we are straying, but if we do not listen to God, why would we listen to others? This is the easiest question to answer. Satan has made our ears deaf to the truth. We must keep in consent communication with God, and not only when there is a problem in our life. This will assure that we act the way God wants and demands from us.

Among my people are found wicked men who lie in wait, like men who snare birds and like those who set traps to catch men.

(Jeremiah 5:26) NIV

WHAT IF?

What if - God's directions does not matter?

What if - there is no heaven?

What if - there is no salvation?

What if - Jesus did not die for our sins?

What if - your sins do not matter?

What if - you do not care about loved ones?

What if - you keep making bad decisions in life?

What if - you are being deceived?

What if - your friends are using you?

What if - God does not love you?

What if - you avoid help?

What if - ....?

What if you are wrong about one or all of these? Not only will you be hurting yourself, but hurting the people in you life that matters. The people in your life care about you. They love and respect you and don't want to see any harm come to you. God gave you these love ones and friends as a gift, because of His love for you. You will encounter evil people that will seem like friends and love ones. They will try to interfere with your relationship with God, loved one and friends. Seek the truth through the Word of God.

Why do you boast of evil, you mighty man?
Why do you boast all day long,
you who are a disgrace in the eyes of God?
(Psalm 52:1) NIV

What is the awful noise?

Have you ever heard fifty band members warming up? It sounds like tin trashcans rolling down the street…it's an awful noise. Each person is trying to set their own instrument and timing. When you put all fifty members in the assigned location and they start performing, it sounds great. These fifty members didn't just show up one day and make music. It takes individual and group practice for them to come together and sound like a band. This also takes organization and planning. God does not make us do planning or organization to find salvation. All He asks of us is to believe in Him and have faith. Salvation is granted to us in that second. We must have the seed of the Lord planted within us and from that second on; it grows and keeps growing. When we start our Christian life, we also may sound like tuning an instrument. As we grow with Christ and His family, we become one of the band members. We become a member of the Christian family of God. With God as our bandleader, we make wonderful music for the heart and soul.

> Four thousand are to be gatekeepers and four thousand are to praise the LORD with the musical instruments I have provided for that purpose."
>
> (1 Chronicles 23:5) NIV

WHAT TWO LAWS?

People go through life telling others and themselves that they are followers of Christ. They say that they accepted Jesus Christ in their life. They say their life is dedicated to the Lord. Some do and some don't go to church for fellowshipping with other Christians. We as Christians must walk in the Spirit as it is written in the Bible. God directs us to follow the laws of man and most important is the Law of God. The Law of God directs us to everlasting salvation to the kingdom of God. We should not have any questions about what two laws after reading the Bible.

So I say, live by the Spirit, and you will not gratify the desires of the sinful nature. For the sinful nature desires what is contrary to the Spirit and the Spirit what is contrary to the sinful nature. They are in conflict with each other, so that you do not do what you want. But you are led by the Spirit, you are not under the law.

The acts of the sinful nature are obvious: sexual immortality, impurity and debauchery; idolatry and witchcraft; hatred, discord, jealousy, fits of rage, selfish ambition, dissensions, factions and envy; drunkenness, orgies, and the like. I warn you, as I did before, that those who live like this will not inherit the Kingdom of God.

But the fruit of the Spirit is love, joy, peace, patience, kindness, goodness, faithfulness, gentleness and self-control. Against such things there is no law. Those who belong to Christ Jesus have crucified the sinful nature with its passions and desires. Since we live by the Spirit, let us keep step with the Spirit. Let us not become conceited, provoking and envying to each other.

(Galatians 5:16 - 5:26) NIV

What's Your Problem?

We will all encounter problems in our life. It could be illness, work, friends, family, or money. The way we go about dealing with these problems could be the cause of more severe problems. Christians sometimes forget that the Lord is our Shepherd and He will lead us. We think that our problem is not that big and we can handle it ourselves without bothering the Lord. Failure to follow God's wishes only allows Satan the chance to take control and then we will have major problems. There should be no question in a Christian's mind if they are acting in the Lord's direction. The problem is that Satan will attempt to disguise his words, letting you think they are God's Words. God does not ever cause us to act evil toward others; this is the work of Satan. When we do encounter problems within our life, we must trust in the Lord and listen to what He is telling us. We must surrender our problems to Him. We must trust in God's spiritual intervention and not ignore the truth of His Word.

1 The wise woman builds her house,
but with her own hands the foolish one tears hers down.

2 He whose walk is upright fears the LORD,
but he whose ways are devious despises him.

3 A fool's talk brings a rod to his back,
but the lips of the wise protect them.

4 Where there are no oxen, the manger is empty,

but from the strength of an ox comes an abundant harvest.

5 A truthful witness does not deceive,
but a false witness pours out lies.

6 The mocker seeks wisdom and finds none,
but knowledge comes easily to the discerning.

7 Stay away from a foolish man,
for you will not find knowledge on his lips.

(Proverbs 14:1 – 14:7) NIV

Where Am I?

Have you ever been on a trip and become lost? The first thing you need is to find out where you are. If you know where you are, you then can figure out how to get there. Sometimes we do not want to ask anyone for help and we try to find our own way. This may work on some occasions, but not always. This type of attitude may get us even more lost. We may think that it is no big deal being lost and that were not going to fall off the face of the earth. Christians should not have the attitude that it is the big deal if we sin. All we have to do is ask God for forgiveness. How could we think that we are a Christian with that type of attitude? Christians do not act this way by committing a sin. They know God will forgive them. Christians will sin, as that is human nature, but to sin intentionally is not being a Christian. Where we are as a Christian, should not be a question we ask ourselves. A Christian that follows the word of God is one who has peace of mind, knowing that he is not lost.

You, however, are controlled not by the sinful nature, but by the spirit. If the spirit of God lives in you and if anyone does not have the spirit of Christ, he does not belong to Christ.

(Romans 8:9) NIV

WHERE THE FOOTSTEPS GO

Think about all the steps we take in our lifetime as a Christian. When the ground is covered with snow, all our steps leave footprints that show where we came from. If someone is following us, they can use the prints in the snow to go the same way as we traveled. Think about all the great places we go that we would love people to follow our steps. Places such as to fellowship study, church and other places that we serve God! Others always look upon Christians as an example to follow. This should be not hard for us because we have the fruit of the Holy Spirit in our heart and soul. What type of message would we be sending if we falter and visit places that are not within the guidelines of being a Christian? We could think that no one will see us because we will be careful not to be seen and if we are— what is the big deal? The big deal is the fact that we could cause someone to stumble; they could think that if it's all right for us, then they can do the same thing. We are not only responsible for our own actions but of those around us that we could influence. As Christians, we must at all times be an example to others.

> Do not cause anyone to stumble, whether Jews, Greeks or the church of God - even as I try to please everybody in every way. For I am not seeking my own good but the good of many, so that they may be saved. Follow my example, as I follow the example of Christ.
>
> (1 Corinthians 10:32 - 10:33) NIV

WHY DO YOU NOT ANSWER ME?

Why do you not answer my prayers? Am I not a Christian that follows Your word? Lord, I need Your help and You do not respond. What have I done, for You not to help me? Must I do something other then pray for You to answer me? Lord, have I not followed Your Words? Lord, my heart is heavy with questions and I do not know what to do. Please show me what I need to do. Please Lord, do not turn your back to me. Lord if I have offended you, please forgive me. Please Lord, come into my heart and soul with your love and guidance. I beg of You, please forgive me for I was lost and now I want to be found. Please answer my questions and I shall put Your words into practice. You are my Lord and God. I seek everlasting life with You.

"Why do you call me, 'Lord, Lord,' and do not do what I say? I will show you what he is like who comes to me and hears my words and puts them into practice. He is like a man building a house, who dug down deep and laid the foundation on rock. When a flood came, the torrent struck that house but could not shake it, because it was well built. But the one who hears my words and does not put them into practice is like a man who built a house on the ground without a foundation. The moment the torrent struck that house, it collapsed and its destruction was complete."

(Luke 6: 46-49) NIV

WHY DO YOU LOVE ME?

My love for you is unconditional no matter what!

REASON 1: You are part of my heart and soul.

REASON 2: You are beautiful while you sleep.

REASON 3: Your voice is pleasing to me.

REASON 4: Your love for me shines like a sunny day.

REASON 5: You have a caring heart for others.

REASON 6: You speak the words of truth.

REASON 7: You are faithful in your beliefs.

REASON 8: You think of me before yourself.

REASON 9: You inspire others to be like you.

REASON 10: You are you and no one can replace you.

Know therefore that the LORD your God is God; he is the faithful God, keeping his covenant of love to a thousand generations of those who love him and keep his commands.

(Deuteronomy 7:9) NIV

WHY HAVEN'T YOU LEARNED?

Why do you seek the life of a moth?
Is not the moth a plain creature without colors?
Does not the moth seek the light in the darkness, and
        when the light is found does it not fly into the fire and die?
Why do you seek the life of the past?
Have I not shown you My light of everlasting life?
Have I not forgiven you of your past?
Why do you let the past haunt you?
Have I not shown you the life of a butterfly, with its
        wonderful colors and the sweet nectar for its food?
Why do you try to act like a butterfly in the darkness
        where there is no nectar?
Why do you not hear Me?
Why do you let the evil one deceive you in
        your thoughts?

Why do you seek that of life without colors? Have I not given you the colors of the sunrise and sunset? Do you not enjoy the rays of the sun? Why do you seek the darkness with the moths? Do you not have My word in you? Do not let the evil one deprive you of My gifts. I have given you the nectar of everlasting life, not the light of destruction. I have not left you, My child. I am here with you, listen to My words and not that of the evil one. Come to Me for the nectar of life.

The Lord is far from the wicked but he hears the prayers of the righteous.

(Proverbs 15:29) NIV

123

WITHOUT PRACTICE

Have you ever heard the saying "practice makes it perfect?" Practice at anything takes time, energy and patience for us to master what we are practicing. Perfect is only what God can do. We use the word perfect to our standards. Most of the time when we practice at something, we will stop when we think we are at the best we can do. In some cases, we just give up without trying harder and continuing to practice. We take on commitments in life, like being a Christian, parent, or a spouse. If we think any of these are going to be easy and without problems, standby because we are wrong. From the minute we make a commitment until the day we die, we are still practicing and working at it. We can say stop we've done enough, or even worse, just quit. God did not say when He had enough of our sinning He would quit on us. So why do we think we should quit on others and ourselves? God gives us the fortitude to keep us going. All we need to do is follow Him. Before we quit on ourselves, ask for help from the Lord. So go out and shake off that "I quit or I've done enough" attitude and practice with God as your instructor.

There is no fear in love. But perfect love drives out fear, because fear has to do with punishment. The one who fears is not made perfect in love

(1John 4:18) NIV

Wouldn't That Be Great?

God has promised us everlasting life and salvation with Him. The only requirements are that we accept Jesus Christ as our savior and know that He died on the cross for all of our sins. With this acceptance, we receive the Holy Spirit and all of God's gifts. God intended for us to be happy during our short time here on earth. He promises us unyielding happiness when we enter into heaven. We will make many choices throughout life that can affect our happiness. One of the biggest and most important choices we make is whom we choose to spend our life with. Christians look for that special person that we can share the word of God and all the wonderful gifts with. We sometimes blind ourselves with the wants of the flesh and not the needs of our spirit. We as Christians need to grow with the spirit of God. By having that special person in our life, we grow as one in the eyes of the Lord. We will meet many people throughout our lifetime and when God chooses that one special person for us, we will know it. If the fruit of the Spirit is with us and it is God's will, no man can stand in the way. May God our Father send each of us that special person.

Now we have received not the spirit of the world but the Spirit who is from God, that we may understand what God has freely given us.

(1 Corinthians 2:12) NIV

BIOGRAPHY

THOMAS GARTON

I was born and raised on the east coast. I was attending a vocational high school when the spirit hit me to join the Navy. I retired after serving twenty years to my country. I had the privilege and opportunity to travel and live throughout this great country and the world. I now reside with my wife Deb and our children in the wonderful state of Wisconsin.

It was not until early 2002 when I found the Lord and all His glory. This may sound like a dream, but it's the truth. I am a very scheduled and detailed person when it comes to being on time, whether it is for work, an appointment or any occasion. My day starts out just like thousands of others; wake up, get ready for work, leave, and be at work on time. The day I found the Lord was a special day, although very unusual for me. I did my usual routine or so I thought. When I arrived at work, I noticed that the parking lot was full. Normally there is only a hand full of cars there at that time in the morning. Walking in I noticed the time and, to my unbelief, I was over an hour late. This hit me like a ton of bricks. I know that I had been having trouble in my life but being late was not one of them. To this day, I still cannot account for that lost time. I managed through the day and on the way home, I tried to tell myself that this was no big thing. When I arrived home, I went to my workshop to find an automotive book. I came across my Bible, and started to look through it. This was the start of my life with the Lord. I had never written anything before and a book was the farthest thing from my mind, however the Lord was within me and I began writing devotions that very day.

Tate Publishing & *Enterprises*

Tate Publishing is commited to excellence in the publishing industry. Our staff of highly trained professionals, including editors, graphic designers, and marketing personnel, work together to produce the very finest books available. The company reflects the philosophy established by the founders, based on Psalms 68:11,

"the Lord gave the word and great was the company of those who published it."

If you would like further information, please call
1.888.361.9473
or visit our website
www.tatepublishing.com

Tate Publishing & *Enterprises*, llc
127 E. Trade Center Terrace
Mustang, Oklahoma 73064 USA